GREAT
TIME MANAGEMENT
IDEAS

Patrick Forsyth

Marshall Cavendish
Business

CONTENTS

Introduction   I

The ideas

1	See where time goes now	8
2	Plan, work—work, plan	10
3	Setting clear objectives	13
4	Speculate to accumulate	17
5	Using Pareto's law	19
6	Tackling the tyranny of the urgent versus the important	22
7	Give clear instructions	24
8	Beware favorites	26
9	Use a "document parking" system	28
10	Aim at influencing particular result areas	30
11	Make use of checklists	32
12	Use abstracts	34
13	The best assistant	36
14	Communicate with your secretary	38
15	Be brief	40
16	A clear diary	42
17	What kind of system?	44
18	Good, better, best . . . acceptable	46
19	Trust the computer?	48
20	Cancellation as a time saver	50
21	Motivate your people	52
22	Thinking ahead	54
23	See the broad picture	56
24	Avoiding a common confusion	57
25	"Everybody's gone surfing, surfing . . ."	59
26	And let's send a copy to . . .	61

27 Telephone efficiency 63

28 A little help from some "special" friends 65

29 Give yourself some time rules 67

30 Don't write 68

31 Avoid purposeless meetings 70

32 Handling telephone interruptions 72

33 Keep papers safe and tidy 74

34 Do not put it in writing 76

35 A magic word 78

36 The productive breather 80

37 Write faster 82

38 A cosmic danger 84

39 Morning, noon, or night 86

40 Technology to the rescue 88

41 Time to stay put 90

42 When being regular is a problem 92

43 Time to get noticed 94

44 The most time-saving object in your office 95

45 What I meant to say . . . 97

46 Avoiding meeting mayhem 99

47 In the beginning—or not? 101

48 The conflict/time equation 103

49 Too many head chefs 105

50 An idea that generates ideas 107

51 Reward yourself 109

52 Best time for appointments 111

53 But I know where everything is 113

54 One thing at a time—together 115

55 At the bottom of the pile 117

56 Resolve to "blitz the bits" 119

57 "If I had wanted it tomorrow I would have asked for it tomorrow" 121

58 Be secure 123

59	Where you are may be as important as what you do	125
60	Do a swap	127
61	Food for thought	129
62	Less in touch, more time	131
63	In times of (travel) trouble	133
64	While you were away	135
65	"Well, it's always been done like this"	137
66	I was just passing	139
67	Encourage and help others	141
68	To meet or not to meet . . .	143
69	Categorize to maintain the balance	145
70	On occasion, let's talk	147
71	Well spotted	149
72	Fighting the plague	151
73	Let the plant grow	152
74	Over to you	154
75	Know when to leave well alone	156
76	Is that the time?	158
77	Making it clear	160
78	Soldiering on	162
79	Driven to distractions	164
80	A clear agenda = a shorter meeting	166
81	The most time-saving phrase in the English language	168
82	Work to rule!	171
83	A balancing act	173
84	Avoid duplicating information unnecessarily	175
85	The right methodology?	177
86	Make skills save time	179
87	Timing and meetings	181
88	Plan your journey	183
89	Working the plan	186
90	Allow for the unexpected	188
91	So cats can play	190

92 Coping with IT change   192
93 Time to tell a white lie?   194
94 On the move   196
95 Never compete with interruptions   198
96 Meetings: where to hold them   200
97 A time-aware team   202
98 More possibilities   204
99 Focus on what achieves results   206
100 Follow Sinatra   207

Appendix
1 Chairing a meeting   209
2 Delegating   211

INTRODUCTION

Regret for the things you did can be tempered by time; it is regret for the things you did not do that is inconsolable.

Sidney J. Harris

Time to think

Time is a resource like any other. And an important one, respect for which can boost effectiveness and profitability—so time management is a crucial skill. It can enhance personal productivity, allow you to focus on priorities, and ultimately act directly to improve your effectiveness and hence the overall success of the organization.

The inherent difficulties

So, if time management is so much common sense and so useful, why is not everyone a time management expert? Sadly, the bad news is that it is because time management is difficult (but there is good news to come). The classic author G. K. Chesterton once wrote that the reason Christianity was declining was "not because it has been tried and found wanting, but because it has been found difficult and therefore not tried." So it is too with time management. There is no magic formula, and circumstances—and interruptions—often seem to conspire to prevent best intentions from working out. Some people, perhaps failing to achieve what they want, despair and give up.

This is not an area in which you can allow perfection to be the enemy of the good. Few, if any, of us organize our time perfectly, but some are manifestly better at it than others. Why? Simply, it is that those who are more successful have a different attitude to the process.

They see it as something to work at. They recognize that the details matter. They consider the time implications of everything and they work to get *as close to their ideal of time arrangement as they can.*

Little things do mount up. Saving five minutes may not sound like much use; however, do so every working day in the year (some 230 days) and you save nearly two and a half days! Speaking personally, I could certainly utilize an extra couple of days, no problem. If time can be saved across a range of tasks, and for most people it can, then the overall gain may well be significant. The best basis for making this happen, and the good news factor I promised was to come, is to make consideration of time and its management a habit.

Now, habits are powerful. Those that need changing may take some effort to shift, but once new ones are established, then they make the approaches they prompt at least semi-automatic. The process of getting to grips with managing your time effectively may well take a conscious effort, but by establishing good working habits it is one that gets easier as you go on.

The ubiquitous meeting

Perhaps nothing provides a better example of wasted time than business meetings, especially internal ones. Which of us cannot remember a meeting that we emerged from recently saying, "What a waste of time!"? We all know the feeling, I am sure.

Yet there is surely no reason for it to be like this. Some meetings can and do start on time. I can still remember an early boss of mine asking me to join an important executive committee. I hastened to my first meeting, but could not find it. The scheduled conference room was locked and no one seemed to know where the meeting was being held. Meeting up with my boss later and explaining the problem, I remember he simply looked me straight in the eye and said, "When did you arrive?" The meeting was in the designated conference room—but he had locked the door! I was never late for one of his meetings again, and, barring accidents, nor was anyone else. He not only believed it was important to start on time; he organized things accordingly. The meetings tended to be constructive too.

This is a very good example of the effect of culture and habit within an organization combining to save people significant time. With clear intentions, good timekeeping, and a firm hand on the tiller, as it were, most meetings can be productive.

This attitude and approach can be applied in many areas. Respecting how things must be done if they are to be effective and organizing so that the best way of working becomes a habit for all concerned pays dividends over time.

Plan the work and work the plan

The principles of good time management are not complex. Overall they can be summarized in three principles:

- List the tasks you have to perform.

- Assign them priorities.

- Do what the plan says.

It is the last of these principles that causes problems—and, to some extent, the second as well. The logic is usually clear. For example, in conducting training on presentational skills I am regularly told by participants that there is never enough time to prepare. Yet this is a key task. Skimp the preparation, make a lackluster presentation, and weeks of time and work may go down the drain. Putting the preparation time in the diary, setting aside a clear couple of hours or whatever it takes, and sticking to that in a way that avoids interruptions must be worth while.

Yes, such an approach demands some discipline—more if it is a team presentation and colleagues must clear time to be together—but it can be done, and again it pays dividends.

The investment principle

It is a prime principle of time management that time must be invested to save time in the future. Sound preparation of the presentation may take two hours, but how long is involved in replacing a prospect if a sales presentation to a customer goes wrong? No contest. And the same principle applies to systems; sorting something out so that it works well on a regular basis is also likely to be time well spent.

The last of the three main principles above is the one that needs most effort.

Staying "on plan"

There are two main influences that combine to keep you from completing planned tasks. The first is other people and events, and the second is you—procrastination, and interruptions, are ever present. So what helps with all this and keeps you on track? Sadly, there is no magic formula: no one thing that can be done to turn you into a master time manager.

Success is in a number of details; what makes for the best situation is when your overall attitude makes many of these—in one form or another—into habits. The nature of the process fits this series and the format of this book admirably. The ideas here add up to a complete solution, but they are all valuable in their own right, and those that suit you can be adopted one at a time. Review them, adopt or adapt them, and use them to form new positive time management habits—and, cumulatively, your time management and productivity can be made to steadily improve.

Research shows that, starting from a position where you have not really considered any formal time management, a conscientious review and effort to better your situation can result in an improvement in your time utilization of 10–20 percent. This is true almost regardless of the particular pattern of your work, and it is very significant and worth aiming for—at best you can add as much as a day each week to your effective time!

A major asset

Good time management is a real asset to anyone's productivity and effectiveness. Its good effects and habit can proliferate through a team, a company even, and there is clearly a direct link between personal effectiveness and the achievement of corporate objectives. The potential good effects are positive and broad in their impact. So it is worth exploring the possibilities, instilling the right habits, and avoiding any dilution of your firm intentions. And results increase in an organization where everyone is similarly motivated. So how to summarize?—*Brrr, Brrr*—oh, dear, excuse me, the telephone is ringing. Just start dipping into the ideas—*I'll only be a minute.*

Note: First lesson: Never, ever believe the phrase "I'll only be a minute."

Patrick Forsyth

THE IDEAS

The ideas led to the preparation of this book.

The main criteria involved in selecting them were that the approaches described make sense—i.e., they work—and that they also demonstrate a constructive part of the total task of managing your time.

Many of these ideas are no doubt in use by many different people. With some (many?), although many people regard them as normal, it is also common to see them ignored. Potentially, I believe almost everything documented here can be useful to most executives and managers—it is their usefulness that got them included.

Some ideas are such that they will only be relevant to certain people (for example, some relate to those managing other people), but that is the nature of examples. What matters is whether they can, by their nature, assist you to make changes and do things differently so that your productivity and effectiveness are positively affected. So: do not reject an idea because it does not seem immediately to suit you. Look for how the idea—or just the germ of the idea—might act to influence your work practice and how precisely you might be able to draw on it to deploy an approach in your own situation that will positively affect your work.

The range of ideas is intentionally eclectic. Many of them relate to my own experience and practice; all of them I have observed utilized by a range of different people with whom I have crossed paths in my training and consultancy work. All can potentially teach us something. Some ideas you will be able to use at once; others may, as has been said, prompt thought that leads to action and change. Some may only be interesting, but of no immediate relevance—

sometimes because you are operating that way already. No matter, the process of reading the book is likely to put you in a constructive frame of mind and ultimately that is part of the process of change, a change that can affect you and the whole of the organization for which you work.

Note: The ideas are arranged in an intentionally random order; the book is intended as much as anything to be dipped into. That said, **the first five ideas should be read first as the principles highlighted here influence subsequent ideas**. Note also that a number of ideas relate to various common areas, for example, those concerned with a classic potential time-waster: meetings.

SEE WHERE TIME GOES NOW

Any improvement you may be able to make to your time utilization must surely presuppose that you know where time goes in the way that you work now. Most people define this inaccurately unless they check it out.

The idea

There are two ways to check current practice. The first is to estimate it—guesstimate it might be a better phrase. This is most easily done in percentage terms on a simple pie chart. Decide on the main categories of work that define your job and divide the pie chart into segments. Such categories might include:

- Writing.
- Telephoning.
- Meetings.
- Planning.

And they could be more personal: so in my case they would span specific activities such as conducting training and writing books.

The second way is to use a time log to obtain a much more accurate picture—recording everything you do through the day and doing so for at least a week, longer if you can (the chore of noting things down takes only a few seconds, but must be done punctiliously).

Few, if any, people keep a log without surprising themselves, and the surprises can be either that much more time is spent in some areas than you think, or that certain things take up less time than you think (or they deserve)—mainly the former. Some obvious areas for review tend to come to mind as a result.

In practice

- Again using the simple pie chart, it can be useful as a second stage of this review to list what you would ideally like the time breakdown to be. This puts a clear picture in your mind of what you are working toward. Such a picture might even be worth setting out before you read on here.

- All this gives you something to aim toward and will tell you progressively—as you take action—whether that action is having a positive effect. If all the review points in this book are looked at alongside this information, then you can see more clearly whether you are able to take action to improve things, and whether the points refer to areas that are critical for you.

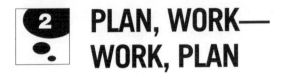

PLAN, WORK— WORK, PLAN

THE WISE SAYING that you should "plan the work, and work the plan" was mentioned in the introduction. Certainly any real progress with time management needs a plan. This must be in writing and must be reviewed and updated regularly; for most people this means a daily check.

The idea

To repeat, the idea here is simply to have a written plan and regularly check and update it.

What is needed is thus sometimes called a rolling plan; not only is it updated regularly, it also provides a snapshot of your workload ahead at any particular moment. As such, it should show accurately and completely your work plan for the immediate future, and give an idea of what lies beyond. As you look ahead, there will be some things that are clear a long way forward—for example, when an annual budget must be prepared and submitted; other areas are less clear and, of course, much cannot be anticipated at all in advance.

At its simplest, such a plan is just a list of things to do. It may include:

- A daily plan.

- A weekly plan.

- Commitments that occur regularly (weekly or monthly or annually).

- A plan for the coming month (perhaps linked to a planning chart).

The exact configuration will depend on the time span across which you work. What is important is that it works for you, that it is clear, that different kinds of activity show up for what they are, and that everything links clearly to your diary and appointment system. How such a list is arranged and how you can use it to improve your work and effectiveness form part of the content of this book, but the existence of the system and the thinking that its regular review prompts is important in its own right. It is the basic factor in creating a time management discipline, and it provides much of the information from which you must make choices—what you do, delegate, delay, or ignore, in what order you tackle things, and so on. Good time management does not remove the need to make decisions of this sort, but it should make them easier and quicker to make and it should enable you to make decisions that really do help in a positive way, so that you get more done and by the best method in terms of achieving your aims.

If this is already beginning to sound like hard work, do not despair. I do not believe that the process of updating and monitoring your rolling plan will itself become an onerous task. It will vary a little day by day, and is affected by your work pattern, but on average it is likely to take only a few minutes. I reckon I keep a good many balls in the air and am a busy person; my own paperwork on this takes perhaps five minutes a day, but—importantly—this prevents more time being taken up in less organized juggling during the day.

In practice

- One point here is crucial. Some people, perhaps most, have a proportion of their day in which action is reactive. Things occur that cannot be predicted, at least individually, and a proportion of the available time is always going to go in this way. Such activity is not automatically unimportant, and the reverse may well be true. For example, a manager on the sales or marketing side of a commercial company may have inquiries and queries coming from customers that are very important and must be dealt with promptly, but will nevertheless make fitting in everything else more difficult. Sometimes the reaction to this is to believe that, because of this reactive element, it is not possible to plan, or to plan effectively. The reverse is true. If your days do consist, even in part, of this sort of random activity, it is even more important to plan, because there is inherently less time available to do the other things that the job involves and that time has to be planned even more thoroughly to maximize its effectiveness.

- Work out what proportion of your day may be like this and then only plan other tasks to fill the time available once the reactive element is completed.

- Everyone needs a plan, everyone can benefit from having a clear view of what there is to be done. If you do not have this, then the work of setting it up will take a moment, but it is worth while and, as has been said, it need not then take long to keep up to date. Once it is in place, you can evolve a system that suits you and that keeps up with the way in which your job and its responsibilities change over time.

3. SETTING CLEAR OBJECTIVES

Any plan is, in turn, as good as the objectives that lie behind it. So it is to objectives, certainly a fundamental factor affecting the management of time, that we now turn.

The idea

Always set objectives. Maxims advocating setting clear objectives are everywhere—for example, the idea that if you don't know where you are going any road will do. The quotation from Lewis Carroll (in *Alice's Adventures in Wonderland*) makes the same point elegantly:

> "Would you tell me, please, which way I ought to walk from here?"
>
> "That depends a good deal on where you want to get to," said the Cat.
>
> "I don't much care where . . ." said Alice.
>
> "Then it doesn't matter which way you walk," said the Cat.
>
> ". . . so long as I get *somewhere*," Alice added, as an explanation.
>
> "Oh, you're sure to do that," said the Cat, "if you only walk long enough."

It is sound advice; you do need clear objectives, and they must not be vague or general hopes.

A much quoted acronym spells out the principles involved: objectives should be SMART, that is: Specific, Measurable, Achievable, Realistic, and Timed. An example will help make this clear. A perennial area of management skill, on which I regularly conduct training, is that body of skills necessary in making formal presentations. (Incidentally, this too is an area with a link to time management. Any weakness in this area will tend to result in longer, and perhaps more agonizing, preparation. Good presentation skills save time. But I digress—back to objectives.)

It is all too easy to define the objectives for a workshop on this topic as being simply to ensure participants "make better presentations," a statement that is unlikely to be sufficiently clear to be really useful. Applying the formula might produce a statement such as:

Objectives for a presentation skills course:

- *Specific*: To enable participants to make future presentations in a manner and style that will be seen as appropriate by their respective audiences, and that will enhance the message they put over and allow them to achieve their purpose.

- *Measurable*: In other words, how will we know this has been achieved? Ultimately, in this case by the results of future presentations; but we might also consider that the trainer or the group, or both, will be able to judge this to a degree at the end of the event by observing the standard during practice.

- *Achievable*: Can this be done? The answer in this case will depend on the prevailing standard before the course. If the people are inexperienced and their standard of presentation is low, then the answer may be that it cannot. If, as we assume for the sake of our developing example, they are people who are of sufficient seniority, experienced, and with some practice in the area of presentations, then the objectives should be achievable—given a suitable amount of time and a suitable program.

- *Realistic*: Picking up the last point, if the time, say, is inadequate, then the objectives may not be realistic. These people can potentially be improved, we might say, but not in one short session.

- *Timed*: "Timed" in training terms will reflect the timing of the course; it may be scheduled to take place in one month's time, so the objectives cannot, by definition, be realized before then. Also the duration: is a one- or two-day (or any other number of days) program going to do the job?

Such an approach is far more likely to provide guidance in the form of clear objectives. Clear objectives really are important, and any lack of clarity can affect every aspect of a person's work, not least time management, sometimes doing so surreptitiously.

In practice

- Much of what needs to be done to manage time effectively is concerned with tackling conflicts and making decisions about what comes first, and none of this is possible if there is no underlying clarity about objectives to act as a reference.

- This is not the place for a detailed review of objectives setting; suffice it to say that this is important to everything in corporate life. An organization functions best with clear corporate objectives, the management structure works best when individual managers are clear about what it is they are expected to achieve and, in turn, they can get the best from staff if they provide clear objectives for them. Consider your own position. Are there any areas that are not clear in this respect? If so, do they make for problems or conflict regarding the way you go about the job? If you answered "yes" to the first question, then you probably did the same for the second.

- Even a simple example makes the point. If a manager is asked to review a system of some sort, it might be for many reasons: to improve accuracy, to speed up operations, to save money, or all three. But undertaking this task is going to take longer if any of this is unclear. In that case, either time needs to be spent working out or checking objectives, or work is put in toward some arbitrary objective that proves inadequate; both end up taking up more time. As it is with one task, so it is with the job overall. If you do not have a clear job description, or if you are uncertain what objectives you should be aiming toward achieving, then check, seek clarification, and managing what you do will at once be easier.

SPECULATE TO ACCUMULATE

A FURTHER POINT, again one touched on in the introduction, needs stating as a useful overall principle. You will find that some ways of saving time, or better utilizing it, do need an investment—but it is an investment of time. It seems like a contradiction in terms, having to spend time to save time. Again this can all too easily become a barrier to action. Yet the principle is clear.

The idea

Invest time to save time: there is a time equation that can and must be put to work if time is to be brought under control. There are many ways of ensuring that time is utilized to best effect, and, while some take only a moment, others take time either to set up or for you to adopt the habit of working in a particular way.

If we consider an example, then the point becomes clear. This is linked to delegation, a subject we return to later, and to the phrase you have perhaps said to yourself, or that at any rate is oft repeated: "It is quicker to do it myself." When this thought comes to mind, sometimes, and certainly in the short term, the sentiment may well be correct. It is quicker to do it yourself. But beware, because this may only be true at the moment something occurs. Say someone telephones you requesting certain information, it doesn't matter what, but imagine that you must locate and look something up, compose a brief comment to explain it, and send the information off to the other person with a note of the comment. It is a minor matter and will take you only four or five minutes.

Imagine further that, to avoid the task, you consider letting someone else do it. They are well able to, but explaining and showing them what needs to be done will certainly take 10–15 minutes of both your time and theirs. It really is quicker to do it yourself. Not so; or rather certainly not so if it is a regularly occurring task. Say it is something that happens half a dozen times a week. If you take the time to brief someone, then they will only have to take the action for less than a week and the time spent briefing will have paid off; thereafter you save a significant amount of time every week, indeed you save time on every occasion that similar requests are made on into the future. This is surely worth while. The time equation here of time spent as a ratio of time saved works positively. This is often the case and worthwhile savings can be made by applying this principle, both to simple examples such as that just stated and to more complex matters where hours or days spent on, say, reorganizing a system or process may still pay dividends.

In practice

- Beware: it is so easy to fall into this trap. For whatever reason, we judge it to be possible (better?) to pause from what we are presently doing for the few moments necessary to get another task out of the way, but not for longer in order to carry out a briefing or whatever other action would rid us of the task altogether, and ultimately make a real time saving. It is worth a thought. Become determined not to be caught in this time trap and you are en route to saving a great deal of time.

5 USING PARETO'S LAW

WORKING EFFECTIVELY MEANS deciding the relative priorities of different tasks. Obvious perhaps, and of course you may say some things are clearly more important than others. But it is very easy to underestimate just how much this concept influences what you need to do, indeed just how much it influences your inherent effectiveness.

Many years ago, the Italian economist Vilfredo Pareto recognized the truism that carries his name and that is now more commonly called the 80/20 rule. It links cause and effect in a ratio and, although this is not represented absolutely accurately in real life, an approximate 80/20 ratio is consistently found in many business activities, sometimes with a precision that is considerable. This means that for instance:

- 20 percent of a company's customers are likely to produce 80 percent of its revenue.

- 20 percent of factory errors are likely to cause 80 percent of quality rejects.

And it applies specifically in terms of issues relating directly to time:

- 20 percent of meeting time results in about 80 percent of decisions made.

- 20 percent of items to read that pass across your desk produce 80 percent of the information you need in your work.

The idea

So you must recognize that just 20 percent of your working time probably contributes around 80 percent of what is necessary for success in your job, and you must reflect this in the way you operate so that attention is focused on those key issues that have this dramatic effect.

In practice

- You may not be able to readily identify exactly which of your tasks have this effect. Some things will be clear, others may need some thought. Have a look at your job description, at how you spend time, and make yourself think through and decide just what it is about what you do that has the greatest effect.

- It may not always be obvious for all sorts of reasons. You may take some key things for granted; for instance, forgetting once they have become a routine how important they are. Certainly you are unlikely to find a direct relationship between such a list of key issues and the things that you spend the most time on. Just this simple review may prompt you to make some changes to your work pattern. Clear objectives and a clear job specification, together with a clear idea of which tasks influence what results and which are key in 80/20 terms, are the only rational bases for deciding priorities. Give yourself this basis and you will be better equipped to work effectively both in terms of time spent on key issues and in terms of reducing or eliminating corresponding minor matters.

Note: Given the right intention, and motivation, it is possible for anyone to improve their time utilization, and perhaps for those who have not given any aspect of time management much conscious thought of late to markedly improve the way they work. However, it takes more than a review of time management and the adoption of one or two ideas to make you truly productive for life. A review will kick-start the process, but the right way of thinking must continue it. The best time managers have not only instilled in themselves good habits and so put part of the process on automatic pilot, as it were; they also view time management as an area of perpetual fine-tuning. In everything they do, the time dimension is considered. It becomes a prerequisite for the various ways in which they work, and they continuously strive to improve still further the way they work and what it allows them to achieve. That fine-tuning too becomes a habit.

With the base principles reviewed up front in mind, all you need now are other areas to work on—from here on, while you may read consecutively if you wish, the order of ideas is random.

Dip in and add things that fit to your "better time management" campaign.

TACKLING THE TYRANNY OF THE URGENT VERSUS THE IMPORTANT

IT CAN SOMETIMES be curiously difficult to decide certain priorities (even with Pareto's law in mind—see Idea 5). Asking why brings us to the vexed question of the urgent versus the important. The urgent and the important are different in nature, yet both generate pressure to deal with them "before anything else."

The idea

It may help to think here of four categories—things that are:

- Urgent and important.

- Important but not urgent.

- Urgent but not important.

- Neither important nor urgent.

Overall, the key is to think first and make considered decisions before letting particular circumstances push you into doing anything first, or just trying to do everything. Things that need action taking fast you must then either do, or delegate, at once. Things that will wait should not just be put on one side, but scheduled so that they get the time they deserve and are also completed.

In practice

- The principle described above may seem difficult; indeed, it *is* difficult. But the difficulty is, at least in part, psychological.

We usually know what is most in need of action, yet somehow the pressures of circumstances combine to give some things an "unfair"—and inappropriate—advantage and we allow that to dictate the decision and give something priority. This is a prime area where resolve is more important than technique, where there is no magic formula, and making the right judgments in a considered way must become a habit if we are to remain organized in the face of such pressures.

GIVE CLEAR INSTRUCTIONS

THERE IS AN old saying that there is never time to do anything properly, but there must always be time to do it again. Nothing is more likely to end up with something having to be redone than a manager not making it clear to people what they had to do in the first place. Communication is not easy, but the responsibility for getting it right is with the communicator—and that, if you are issuing instructions, is you. Similarly, if people do not really understand and fail to query it, perhaps because they are worried you will blame them, then that is also your fault because you should make sure things are clear and encourage people to ask if necessary.

The idea

Always ensure that instructions are clear. People should be told:

- *What* needs to be done (and give them sufficient details).

- *Why* it needs to be done (knowing the objectives may make the task clearer and will improve motivation).

- *How* it should be done (methodology etc.).

- *When* it should be completed (and anything else about the timing).

In practice

- Instructions should always include asking if everything is clear—get some feedback. Any short cut of this sequence must be on the basis of genuine knowledge or familiarity, not simply assumption that all will be well. Good, clear instructions save time, written guidelines do the same, and for some tasks they are useful; this is especially true of awkward or difficult jobs that are performed regularly but infrequently.

- One such job in my office is changing the toner unit on the laser printer: no one remembers exactly how to do it next time it is necessary, and retaining and consulting the instructions saves time. Moral: all instructions, in whatever form, must be clear. If you issue instructions, remember this; if you receive them—ask if necessary.

8 BEWARE FAVORITES

THIS MAY SEEM an odd one, but it is potentially even more time-wasting than putting off things that you do not like or that you find difficult. Many people spend a disproportionate amount of time on the things they like doing best and, perhaps, also do best. This is perfectly natural and there are various reasons for it. An important one is that any concentration on what you like is what seems to produce the most job satisfaction. This is fine if that satisfaction comes simply from doing whatever it is and the thing itself is necessary, though the danger is that you may be prone to some over-engineering, doing more than is necessary, putting in more time and sometimes producing a standard of quality or excellence that is just not necessary.

But there can be more sinister reasons for this practice. For example, it may be because:

- You are using one task to provide an excuse to delay or avoid others (difficult or unfamiliar things, perhaps), telling yourself, with seeming reason, that you are too busy to get to them.

- You are concerned about delegating (a subject covered separately) and worry that a task is not a candidate for this, so you go on doing it yourself and go on over-engineering.

- You find the work conditions of one task too tempting, such as a low-priority job that involves visiting an attractive location new to you, for instance; this is something that is compounded by the opposite being true of the priority task.

- You find some aspect of the task fun; as an example, this happens to some people who have a fascination with computers, and they spend hours devising, say, a graphic representation of some figures when something simpler would meet the case just as well.

All these and other reasons can cause problems. The practice is frankly all too easy to engage in, we are all prone to it, probably all do it to some extent, and thus we all have to be constantly on our guard against it. Usually it continues because it is easy not to be consciously aware that it is happening.

The idea

Avoid what is sometimes called "cherry picking." The answer here is to really look, and look honestly, as you review your tasks and your regular work plan for examples of this happening. Better still, look for examples of where it might happen and make sure that it does not. Of all the points in this book, I would rate this as in the top few best potential time savers for most people. Do not be blind to it—it is so easy to deny it happens. Check it out and see how much time you save. And, who knows, maybe some of the extra things you can then fit in will become tomorrow's favorite tasks.

In practice

- Self-generated interruptions can be surprisingly time-consuming and their frequency can be one of the surprises that often emerge from keeping a personal time log. It is easy to be blind to them and, at the risk of being repetitive, it is logical to watch for these before the ones involving other people or outside circumstances as their cause.

USE A "DOCUMENT PARKING" SYSTEM

PROBLEM: YOU MAY have many things on the go at any one time, and in physical terms they may be represented by a single sheet of paper or a batch of correspondence. Many of them do not need action, or rather nothing can be done immediately. Such items are what so often constitute the ever-present pending tray that makes many a desk groan under its weight. The net result is that you spend a great deal of time either shuffling through the heap to locate things, or checking things in there to see what you might in time do about them.

The nature of some of the material makes the problem worse. Say one item can only be dealt with when certain monthly performance figures are published; in that case, to keep checking may well be both time-consuming and useless, as no action can be taken until a later stage anyway. Further, constant reviewing can achieve little in advance of knowing what the figures say, as there are many different possibilities in terms of what they might predicate.

The idea

If you suffer this sort of situation, you need a parking place for such things, somewhere safe yet guaranteed to trigger prompt action at the appropriate moment. You need what is called a Prompt (or Bring Forward) File. This means you take an item and decide when you will be able to progress it. This may be at a specific time (when the monthly figures arrive), or it may not (just six weeks on, or longer, at the start of the next financial year). Then you simply mark it with the date on which you next want to see it and file it, with other similar items, in date order. Then forget it. Waste no more time even thinking about it. You do not have to, because every day you, or your secretary, can check the file and take out anything marked with that day's date. At which point you can either act or, occasionally, give something another date and move it forward.

In practice

- A couple of provisos must be borne in mind. First, you may want to limit the total quantity of items (or A–Z list them) as something will happen occasionally that means you need to take action earlier than you thought, and you will need to retrieve an item from the file and action it ahead of the date you originally set. Second, you may want to link it to a diary note, especially if you have no secretary. This is a simple, easy to set up, common-sense idea that works for many people.

AIM AT INFLUENCING PARTICULAR RESULT AREAS

EVERYTHING YOU DO in time management terms is designed to effect efficiency, effectiveness, and productivity; to enable you to do more and to do everything better than would otherwise be the case, so as to achieve the results your job demands. But there are advantages to be gained en route to these ends, and these are useful in their own right.

The idea

Considering and keeping specific advantages in mind can help you adopt some of the methodology necessary to an organized way of working and make the whole process easier. Such advantages include:

- Having a clear plan, knowing and having an overview of what must be done—the first step to successfully completing the tasks on your list. Such clarity will make adequate preparation more likely and this can reflect directly on achievement.

- Having a clear link between things to do and overall objectives, which is a sound recipe for keeping on track.

- Being better organized (e.g., not wasting time looking for things).

- Your memory coping better with what you actually need to remember (the systems take care of some of this for you, and it is not necessary to keep everything in your head).

- Being better able to identify and concentrate on the essentials.

- Wasting less energy on irrelevancies.

- Making better decisions about how things should be done (and better business decisions generally).

- Better coordination of tasks (progressing certain things in parallel saves time).

- Having a greater ability to cope with or remove distractions and interruptions.

- Cultivating the habit of greater self-discipline about time matters, which makes consistency of action progressively easier.

- A greater ability to cope with the unexpected and emergency elements of any job.

Any of these are useful, but some may be more useful to you than others, at least at a particular moment.

In practice

- It may be useful to look for the particular advantage you want: wasting less energy on irrelevancies or, more specifically, attending fewer meetings, for example. Or you may wish to adopt methods that suit you precisely. This is not to say that all those listed above do not have a good general effect on productivity. They do. Focusing what you do carefully will enable you to achieve more, and get greater satisfaction from the results you do achieve.

- Additionally, you may have more time to develop what you do and how you do it, and motivate yourself (and staff you may have), all of which can potentially improve things still further. All this may also remove some of the things that create the feeling that a job is "hard work." "Working hard" is nearly always a prerequisite of success, but you do not want tasks to constantly be like trying to nail jam to the wall when a little organization will ensure they go smoothly.

MAKE USE OF CHECKLISTS

EVEN ROUTINE TASKS can give pause for thought. If you do something wrong or incompletely in respect of some detail, how much time does that waste?

The idea

To avoid those pauses for thought—*How does this go?*—and, more important, to remove the necessity to do something again or the cost or inconvenience of not having it complete, consider the role of checklists.

Even a tiny number of cases of uncertainty may make more checklists something that will save time.

In practice

- Consider an example: many companies have a form that is completed when a sales inquiry is received. Completing such a form does not only create a record and act as a prompt to further action; it can also act as a checklist, for instance reminding someone to:

  - Check the inquirer's job title as well as name.

  - Ask how they heard of the company or product.

  - Refer to an account number.

- There might be many such items involved. Many such routine tasks are not both routine and predictable, just as the conversation with the customer may take all sorts of routes and it is easy to forget those questions that might be considered optional, or at least of lesser importance. So a checklist helps. This can be either a form designed to be completed and acting in this way as the completion proceeds, or as a point of reference, literally just a note of what should be done. They can be originated by an individual or department or be an overall organization standing instruction.

- All sorts of things lend themselves to this sort of approach; you may like to make a mental note to look, in particular, at things that provide assistance outside your own area of expertise. For instance, if you are a dunce with figures, but occasionally have to undertake some marginal costing, keep the "crib sheet" that helps you do it safely to hand.

12 USE ABSTRACTS

WE LIVE IN an information age. But keeping in touch and up to date can be a chore. No one needs reminding of the amount of reading there is to do in most jobs. For some it is very important to keep up to date with the technical area their job involves; for others management processes themselves are worth regular study. In both cases the first task is to decide which, from the plethora of published information, should command your attention. This first selection exercise can be time-consuming of itself before you actually study anything individually.

The idea

But help is at hand. In most fields it is possible to subscribe to what are called abstract services. These are not expensive, and from them you receive a regular list of what has been published on a given subject. Such a list does not just contain the titles of articles or papers (and books), but details of the authors, and, most important, synopses of the content. It is this latter information that lets you select with reasonable accuracy those items you judge you want to look at in more detail. You can then either turn up the source and read the item in full (scanning it first, no doubt) or, sometimes, the service will provide—sometimes for a small fee—a copy of a particular article without your having to purchase the full magazine or journal in which it appears.

In practice

- If the thought of this facility appeals to you, then you may want to check what services are available that are relevant to you and your job. Typically they will come from libraries, colleges, trade associations and professional bodies (e.g., management institutes), business schools, and the like. If you find something that offers a service that appears to suit you, then it is perhaps worth taking out a trial subscription to see whether it does save you time. If you find it does, and if it also helps you find information you might otherwise miss, it can then be economic to continue, in which case you have another continuing time saver on your side.

- Many abstract services are available online these days and perhaps the first place to check is suitable websites (many of which provide free information).

THE BEST ASSISTANT

THERE IS AN old story told of a secretary to a very senior executive who was a frequent traveler. Asked by someone if he could see him, she replied that she was sorry but he was in Hong Kong. "Abroad again," the visitor replied. "He's always overseas. Tell me, who does all his work while he's away?" She looked him straight in the eye and answered without hesitation: "The same person who does it when he's here." Some secretaries perhaps have such authority, but while the secretary is not a panacea, a good one can certainly help.

The idea

In the modern workplace secretaries are less common than was once the case. But for those who have one, a good secretary can not only be the recipient of some of your delegation; they can also act as a regular prompt to good time management and take a genuinely active role in organizing you, or your whole department.

The emphasis here is on a good secretary (but the principle applies to anyone in an assistant role, male or female), so the first job is to find the right one for you; and then, as we will see, work with her to create the end result you want.

In practice

So, what makes the right secretary/PA?

- The characteristics of the ideal secretary are legion. As well as typing, and sometimes shorthand, skills, she (the classic "secretary" is still most usually a she) must be familiar with an increasing array of office technology. In addition, it helps if she is patient, is gifted with second sight, and has two pairs of hands. But what of time management? Whether she has a natural or acquired organizational ability is difficult to assess at an interview, as is whether she really cares about such things. If, however, you can make such an assessment, and are able to appoint a candidate who has characteristics of this sort, then you will have a real asset on board in your battle to win the time war.

- When recruiting, ask any questions you can think of that will give you information in this area, particularly about past experience in managing the diary, appointments, and projects of those she has worked for previously. This is also something to check in taking up references (always a wise precaution).

- There are two other important characteristics that you should seek. First, that she will work your way. This is essential as there may be existing procedures and systems, as well as management style, that you need her to fit in with; on the other hand, always be ready to learn from her. There is no monopoly on good ideas, the only criterion being that the ideas are useful. Second, that she has sufficient "weight" or clout; that is, she must be able to stand up for you with colleagues and others, to say "no" on your behalf, and to make requests on your behalf—and make them stick.

- Achieve this and your attempts to control your time will have a permanent ally: one who will work with you to achieve what you want and who will, at best and with experience, take an active role in the process. One final point—if you share a secretary or assistant, this does not negate what is said here, though achieving an operational consensus may take a moment and some sensible collaboration.

14 COMMUNICATE WITH YOUR SECRETARY

It is not much use having a good secretary (or assistant), one who is sympathetic to time management, and then not communicating with her (note that management, motivation and more are necessary too).

The idea

Communicate: there may seem never to be time for this, but if you do find the time for it, then it will help you save much more time than this communication takes. Many executives start the day with a meeting with their secretary, perhaps when the mail arrives in the morning. You must decide what suits you best and also work out a way of keeping in touch and up to date with her if you spend much time out of the office, though modern communications make this easier than once was the case.

In practice

- Your secretary must know how you work and know what you have on the go at any particular time. And she should, if possible, share your view of priorities, knowing what you are prepared to be interrupted for, which things and people rate most time and attention, and which tasks come first. You need to review and organize the diary together, and over time it helps if you explain what you are doing and why so that she gets to know some of the detail beyond her own personal duties. Once she has some experience, more may well be possible. She can take the initiative on things, accompany you to certain meetings, and ultimately run whole areas of your office life in a way that increases your utilization of time dramatically. Find areas of real responsibility, let her look after them and make the decisions affecting them, and it can pay dividends.

- Communication is the one prerequisite for creating a good working relationship. If lack of communication causes problems—a string of time-wasting meetings in your diary as you come back from a trip, say—then consider the fault yours. Communicate clearly and regularly, and remember that includes listening.

15 BE BRIEF

CLEARLY, BREVITY IN communications saves everybody time; for you in writing something, for the recipient in reading it.

The idea

The idea here is simple (and can be stated in a line and a half): Be brief. Do not succumb to verbal diarrhea and keep things simple. Easy?

In practice

- The pressures of the modern workplace and the almost universal use of email have forced us into better practice with regard to brevity. But there is a caveat. However brief, messages must be clear.

- If brief, your written communication may be less time-consuming to create, but any misunderstandings it may give rise to will just jack up the time involved as things are sorted out. So, choosing my words carefully, you need to be succinct and precise and, of course, clear (this is not the place for a treatise on making communications understandable, but communication should never be assumed to be easy; it is often the reverse, and misunderstandings must be responsible for a massive amount of wasted time when things must be queried and clarified).

- So this is worth a (fittingly) short point here. I know I would prefer to receive shorter rather than longer messages provided the information is clear. I do not have to wade through any extraneous material and it saves me time. If it takes less time to write, it can still be perfectly polite, and so if it can be said in three lines then say it in three lines. Beyond that, consider the time saving of three-page memos reduced to one page, reports of ten pages instead of 20 . . . but I promised this would be a short paragraph. Enough said; point made.

16 A CLEAR DIARY

However well organized you may be or get to be, you cannot hope to keep all the details of what you will do when in your head.

The idea

A good, clear diary system is a must. Many formal systems combine the conventional diary with their sophisticated version of the "to do" list. One thing that certainly works well, and which a loose-leaf system allows, is to have at one opening of a binder a complete picture of your day, showing both appointments and things to do. Thus you might allocate a couple of hours to write a report.

What form it takes is a matter of choice; though bear in mind the concept of a "master diary": one place needs to have the definitive record if you are to avoid coming into the office with an appointment to list and finding that someone has double-booked you.

In practice

Small things have an effect on efficiency. The diary should:

* Show full details, certainly full enough to be clear. An entry that reads 'R. B. Lunch' tells you little—where is it, at what time is it, can you be contacted while you are out, how long will it last, and, not least, are you even going to remember in three weeks' time to whom R. B. refers? If you want a real horror story, I know of a case where all it said in someone's diary was the name of a town, with two days ruled out. He was away, presumably staying at a hotel, and had only told his family to contact him via his office. When one of his children was involved in an accident, it took two

days before the message reached him. His diary was a copybook example of clarity thereafter.

- Show how long is set aside for things (this will help you and others decide what else can be fitted in).

- Schedule all (or most) of your working time rather than just appointments, perhaps the most important and useful difference between just an appointments diary and a time management system. The two additions are tasks, actually setting aside time to work on a specific project, and thinking time so that creative work is not carried out, as so often happens, only in gaps that are left between appointments. If this is done—leaving space for the unexpected or reactive part of the work, whatever proportion that is—and linked to the concept of a rolling plan, you will stay more organized and be able to judge much better how things are progressing, whether deadlines will be met and tasks completed.

- Be completed in pencil so that alterations can be made without creating an illegible mess.

Two final points. First, the diary is a vital tool, to be guarded and treated with respect. A conventional diary is also therefore a good place to keep other key information, telephone numbers, and other data you need at your fingertips, provided you do not overburden it so that it becomes too thick and unmanageable. Second, the computer, and a variety of electronic personal organizers, are taking over some of these activities. Often this works well. Being able to set up a meeting with six colleagues, some in different cities, at the touch of a button on a networked system may well save time.

For many people a personal diary or planner, in the old sense of something that works anywhere there is a pencil, will always be a part of what helps them work effectively. Certainly the thinking that needs to be applied to diary organization is the same however the information involved may be recorded.

WHAT KIND OF SYSTEM?

Many books on the subject of time management are closely linked to some specific proprietary time management system, consisting of diaries, files, binders, and in some cases more besides. Some even claim that the only route to time efficiency lies with the particular system they recommend. Now this may be fine if the system suits you, but I would suggest caution in taking up any particular system.

No one system is recommended here; I do not in fact use such a branded system myself. This is not to say that I disapprove of them. One of the most organized people I know uses one and swears by it; but I also know people who are the very opposite of organized despite the fact that their desks are adorned with the binders and card indices of their chosen system, so they certainly offer no kind of panacea. Many are restrictive—that is, they can only be used in a particular way and that may well not suit you and how you think and work. There is thus a real danger that if you use a system and some element of it does not work for you, then your use of the whole system falters.

The idea

A better way is perhaps to work out what you need first: what kind of diary, how much space for notes, how many sections to fit the way your tasks are grouped, what permanent filing. Then, when you have thought through what you need and worked that way for a while (a process that will almost certainly have you making a few changes in the light of how things actually work), you can check out the systems and see whether any of them formalize what you want to do and, as they can be expensive, get one knowing that the investment is worth while.

In practice

- The world is full of people who organize themselves perfectly well with no more than a diary, a notebook, or a file. To end this section with something of a recommendation, I would suggest a loose-leaf diary system is a good basis for many (something like a Filofax). This combines a neat system with the flexibility to put in exactly what you need, and that is what is most important. After all, it must reflect your plan and it is your time that you want to organize. Such can be desk or pocket sized (and these days you could pick a computer equivalent if you wished).

- That said, I repeat: there is surely no one system that is right for everyone. Even the precise kind of diary layout you choose must be a personal decision based on your needs, and what else is necessary will reflect the way you work. You must decide; I can only state that all my experience suggests that a flexible and thus tailor-made system is likely to be best.

GOOD, BETTER, BEST . . . ACCEPTABLE

IT IS OFTEN the case that time management goes hand in hand with perfectionism. I would certainly not advocate that anyone adopts a shoddy approach to their work, whatever it may be. There is, however, a dichotomy here, one well summed up in a quotation from Robert Heimleur, who said (perhaps despairingly): "They didn't want it good, they wanted it on Wednesday." The fact is it takes time to achieve perfection, and in any case perfection may not always be strictly necessary. Things may need to be undertaken carefully, thoroughly, comprehensively, but we may not need to spend time getting every tiny detail perfect. This comes hard to those who are naturally perfectionists, and it is a trait that many people have, at least about some things.

The idea

It is necessary to strike a balance. There is always a trade-off here, and it is not always the easiest thing to achieve. Often a real compromise has to be made. You have to make decisions about how to do things based on quality, cost, . . . and time.

In practice

- Cost is often crucial in this. It would be easy to achieve the quality of output you want in many things, but only if cost were no object. And in most jobs budget considerations rank high. It is useful to get into the way of thinking about things in these terms, and doing so realistically so that you consider what is necessary as well as (or instead of?) what is simply desirable or ideal. In doing this, there is one key factor that needs to be built in: the significant, and sometimes the largest, cost of your time.

- Consider all the costs of your working on something; the resultant figure may surprise you. Let me repeat: make sure by all means that what must be done to perfection is done in a way that achieves just that. Otherwise make sure you always keep in mind the balance to be struck between quality, cost, and time; if you do not over-engineer quality, seeking a standard that is not in some instances necessary or desirable, then you will surely save time.

19 TRUST THE COMPUTER?

It has become one of the great myths of the IT age that computers will transform office work, and make everything fast and efficient to action. But like other great promises—*Our cheque is in the post*—it is not entirely to be trusted. Now I have nothing against computers and there are things that one cannot now imagine working any other way. And yet . . . there are questions, certainly as far as efficiency and time utilization are concerned, at desk level for the individual executive. There are examples of things now available that manifestly (mostly!) work well. Such include: databases, graphics programs, email, and desktop publishing—all have advantages over equivalents that do not involve computers.

Yet there are systems that for all their cleverness do not fit their role so well. Think of some of the systems you may be frustrated by as a customer, in the bank, with an insurance company, or at a hotel. Take a hotel account as an example. They are, one presumes, efficient for the hotel but many are very difficult for the guest to fathom without a degree in abbreviations. It is customer service that has suffered in this case.

The idea

Think carefully before you agree to computerize something assuming doing so "must make it better."

In practice

- There is another side to computers: you (well, many of us) need expert help to set up many systems (and in some cases to operate them), there is a high capital cost (though this is coming down), and they are all too readily used as an excuse for not doing things (if I had a small coin for every time I have heard someone in a travel agents say, "Sorry, the computer is down," I could travel round the world free). Above all, in the context of our topic here, they take time to set up and the equation of time must be carefully balanced to see what makes best sense. It is beyond our brief here to investigate IT in depth, but many systems, large and small, do not automatically save time—they can have serious downsides.

CANCELLATION AS A TIME SAVER

THIS IS A brief point, and links to the topic of meetings, which crops up in more than one section. There is an issue here that can waste large amounts of time. It is surprising and curious how meetings that are scheduled for a good reason still run even when not only has the good reason gone but everyone knows it has gone. It is difficult to understand. Perhaps someone thinks it is too late to cancel (I would rather hear two minutes before the meeting that it is canceled than turn up and waste time), or they think that it will still be useful as minor matters can be dealt with "as the people are coming together anyway."

The idea

Usually the thinking above is wrong. It is better to cancel the meeting, or postpone it if the main reason for it has not gone away forever. The idea here is simply to do this and not be sidetracked into allowing time to be wasted.

In practice

- This principle is especially true of regular series of meetings. The example of ten meetings being held through a year is the kind of thing where it is often better to schedule ten knowing you are in fact likely only to need eight or nine. The disruption of one dropped is very much less than pulling an extra one together at short notice, and this should become the habit. Never go ahead just because it is "the regular meeting" or you will waste time.

- There is even a case for refusing to use words such as weekly or monthly in the title of a meeting; it can end up prompting meetings that prove useless.

21 # MOTIVATE YOUR PEOPLE

MOTIVATION IS A powerful force. If you are a manager, then it makes people perform better and that saves time.

The idea

Simply stated—the idea is to motivate people. If the team you manage are well motivated, then they will perform better, with less input from you; it is a formula that saves the manager time and makes for an all-round more productive team. The problem is that this does not just happen. It takes some time. Without doing so, however, you will not get the best from people, and that means some time will be wasted. Again, the equation of time here makes sense: the net effect should be a saving.

In practice

- Motivation has been described as a climate and this is not a bad analogy. Just like the climate or the temperature in a room, it is affected by many different things, and the effect can be for good or ill. There is sadly no magic formula for guaranteeing that motivation will be, and will stay, high. You have to look at the motivational implications of things such as the administration and systems with which people work, the way they relate to colleagues and you as supervisor, their feeling of security in the sense of knowing what they have to do and being part of a good team. All these can pull motivation down if they are organized badly or unsympathetically.

- Similarly, there are many influences that boost people's motivation such as the enjoyment of the work and, more particularly, a sense of satisfaction and achievement in doing it and doing it well. All these and more are important—and it is a subject worth some study if you manage others. Try my book *How to Motivate People* (Kogan Page).

- The details of what motivates people are beyond the brief here, but one thing is worth a mention: small things matter. People do not just like to achieve, they like recognition of that to be shown. Yet most people who are busy cannot, in all honesty, put their hands on their hearts and say that they always remember the little things as much as they should. Think about it yourself. Have you said "thank you" or "well done" often enough lately? It matters, people notice and they expect it. You have time for that—and it will save you time.

- Remember, motivation is essentially long term. It's an ongoing process to change attitudes and you should not expect instant results; rather you should see a variety of actions as creating over time a productive team that will then work effectively in all the ways that make your time go further.

THINKING AHEAD

THIS MIGHT APPROPRIATELY be called the opposite of the "if only . . ." school of ineffective time management. Too often managers find themselves in a crisis that would be all too easily resolved if they could wind the clocks back. We surely all know the feeling. "If only we had done so and so earlier," we say as we contemplate a messy and time-consuming process of unscrambling. In all honesty, though the unexpected can happen sometimes, crisis management is all too common . . . and often all too unnecessary. Coping well with crises that are, for whatever reason, upon us saves time; certainly if the alternative is panic.

The idea

If you can acquire the habit of thinking ahead and take a systematic view of things, then you are that much more likely to see when a start really needs to be made on something. If things are left late or ill thought out (and the two can often go together), then time is used up in a hasty attempt to sort things out at short notice. This tends to make any task more difficult and is compounded by whatever day-to-day responsibilities are current at the time.

In practice

- Some people find that to "see" the pattern of future work and tasks in their mind's eye can be difficult. One invaluable aid to this is the planning or wall chart (see Idea 23 for more detail).

- Whatever you do to document things, however, the key is to get into the habit of thinking ahead—at the same time and without disrupting the current day's workload. Anticipating problems and spotting opportunities can make a real difference to the way you work in the short term.

SEE THE BROAD PICTURE

NOT EVERYONE WORKS solely on a day-to-day basis. Many people have to operate in a way that involves keeping in mind a span of time that may be weeks, months, or even years in extent. Here, a particular approach can enhance the practicality of a diary.

The idea

Using a planner element within a diary is very useful. Anyone who needs to take an overview of a period and see how various different things relate one to another is likely to find it invaluable.

In practice

- The mental process of seeing a span of time, rather than thumbing through pages, is really helpful in managing any kind of project. For example, the production of this book spanned many months, involving time allocated to writing, typesetting and printing with tasks such as reading proofs scheduled in along the way. Care here can prevent missed deadlines and that can save more than time.

- Be careful of taking time in duplication. For instance, some people enter everything in three places: a diary, a planning chart, and a separate wall planner. Additional recording may be necessary too, such as a separate chart to plan and monitor people's holidays. If you want to use a planning chart as your sole diary device, why not do so? The key is to keep a handle on the whole of your schedule no matter what length of time this encompasses.

AVOIDING A COMMON CONFUSION

Most people are in agreement about their work situation. In a word, you are busy. There are so many things to do and insufficient time in which to do them all. Furthermore, the picture changes as you watch. Just as you get one thing done and dusted, others join the queue. The mail arrives, you open your email, someone comes up to your desk and asks a favor, the boss says, "This is urgent" . . .

Yet realistically not everything is of the same import. As this book makes clear, we are all struggling with a plethora of interruptions, admin assumes monstrous proportions, and the processes we must go through make a labyrinth look like a walk in the park. But some things are core tasks, and at the end of the day it is those things that contribute directly to achieving the results we are charged with that must be put first.

The idea

The principle here is trite, a cliché, but it is also a truism. The right approach here is itself a major contributor to personal productivity. It is simply that you should:

Never confuse activity with achievement.

Recognizing that there is a difference between what is urgent and what is important must become a reflex for the effective time manager. Diversions, distractions, and peripheral activity of all sorts must be recognized and kept in their place.

In practice

- This must be a permanent state of mind; in effect it is one of the guiding principles that help ensure a productive approach.

- Not only must the positive aspect of this be kept in mind; so must the tendency to rationalize the wrong things for the wrong reason, categorizing something as important when it is not.

Priorities, dealt with elsewhere, must be just that—and the measure of what is a priority must always include the measure: does this link to planned results? One might also ask: will it take you forward? You may be busy, but "being busy" is never an end in itself.

"EVERYBODY'S GONE SURFING, SURFING . . ."

Here's something that has become a real hazard in recent years and must waste uncounted hours in offices around the world. What's that? The internet: or, more specifically, non-work-related surfing.

The idea

The idea is simple: don't engage in non-work-related surfing.

Actually, that needs some discipline and resolve. After all, the internet is a source of information. An hour ago, before writing this, I logged on to Google to get directions to an office at which I have just set a meeting, a company website to check out the kind of business they were in, and another to book an air ticket. All represented a good, time-efficient way of doing these little jobs, but . . . let me be honest, despite the fact that I'm writing about time management, I was tempted. While my Word file was tucked away at the bottom of the screen, all I had to do was click on Favorites and just slip in one more task (there's a book I want to order from Amazon, for instance).

The worst time-waster in this area is probably social websites such as Facebook. Time very quickly disappears as you dip "just once more" into a chat site. And if you doubt the danger and want another thought that might reinforce the truth, it is reckoned that a high percentage of all the hits on pornographic sites are made between 9 a.m. and 5 p.m. when presumably most computer users are at work!

In practice

- Be aware of the likely distraction and resolve to avoid temptation.

- Don't put sites that you may like and use in private into the Favorites file in your work computer.

- Follow your organization's guidelines—rules—about this sort of thing; they are there for a reason.

AND LET'S SEND A COPY TO . . .

EMAIL IS A wonder of the modern age. It has transformed communication to the extent that having my own broadband connection down and being unable to use email from my computer for ten days recently reduced me to a neurotic wreck spending untold amounts of time driving to the nearest wireless access point. But the system wastes a lot of time too. There's the spam that is the bane of all our lives and that . . . no, a digression here on that would overpower the rest of the book. But in other ways the time it wastes is our collective fault.

The idea

There is mention of email elsewhere in the book: here one aspect is worth its own entry. Sometimes more than one person really does need to see a message. But on many occasions people invent spurious reasons. A copy is sent "just in case" someone wants it, or—worse—"just in case someone tells us off for not including them": what some refer to as insurance copies.

So do *not* send unnecessary copies.

The time it takes to consider this is minuscule. And if we are honest the problem is caused simply by lack of thought or outright laziness. It need not happen. If you don't agree and want to email me about this, please do, but don't copy the publisher, the shop where you bought the book, and . . .

In practice

- Think before you copy anyone. Do they really need it? Will they thank you for it?

- Do not use groups of names unthinkingly. One committee I'm on is populated by people all of whom seem to write to one member by clicking on "All." Please—I hope they read this.

- Say something, for goodness sake, if you are being repeatedly copied unnecessarily—send a (polite) note stopping it. That will save time in the long run.

- If everyone adopted a "do-as-you-would-be-done-by" approach to this, everyone would benefit.

27 TELEPHONE EFFICIENCY

IF YOU MAKE any number of telephone calls as part of your job, it can seem unbelievable how much time is wasted dialing, redialing, and holding on the telephone. Much of this time is these days spent listening to a unique and repetitive form of music that has been known to send even the sanest into unreasonable states, and working your way through endless "press this option" sequences. The simplest way of avoiding all this is to get your secretary to obtain calls for you, but her time is valuable too and, besides, fewer and fewer people have one.

The idea

What does make a real difference is a modern telephone. This is a form of new technology I really warm to, not so complicated that it puts you off and with specific features that are real time savers. For example:

- If you have the ability to store all the common numbers you use, this will save you having to dial them—a couple of digits and the phone does the rest.

- Many will also redial (for example, if the chosen number is busy first time) and some will go on and on dialing automatically until they get through.

- A loudspeaker means that if you have to hold on (listening to the music) then your hands are free and work can continue.

In practice

The features of telephones expand with the march of time, and many save time. In addition, you can sometimes reduce the time taken up by the endless options through which it is necessary to run the gauntlet before you get through to who you want.

Two things help:

- Keep a note of the option numbers for organizations you call regularly; you can often press a number as soon as a list starts rather than waiting until the number you want is given.

- Use a website such as www.saynotoo870.com that will guide you to regular numbers rather than the premium lines beloved of so many organizations. This can save you money, of course, but can often also lead to you being able to avoid the time-consuming options selection hurdle.

A LITTLE HELP FROM SOME "SPECIAL" FRIENDS

CLEARLY ANYTHING YOU must get done but do not do yourself will save time. Who can help you? Other sections in the book investigate some possibilities—staff and colleagues, for instance—but who else is available?

The idea

One option is to use, albeit at a cost, one of the concierge services that have sprung up in recent years. What do they do? Well, one of the best known is Quintessentially, which describes itself as the world's leading luxury lifestyle group focused on providing its members with the best things in life. I phoned their offices and Clementine Brown told me, "With thousands of suppliers across the globe, Quintessentially offers an unrivaled worldwide network and is able to offer discounts and added value with only the very best of products and services. Available 24 hours a day, 365 days a year, by telephone or email, Quintessentially's expert fixers are always on hand to help with our members' needs—whether it be securing last-minute hotel reservations, sourcing the hottest music tickets in town, or accessing the most anticipated sporting events."

Since its launch in 2000, Quintessentially has added a portfolio of 14 sister businesses encompassing property, events, wine, art consultancy, and even a modeling agency. They have 44 offices in a host of major cities worldwide including destinations as diverse as Buenos Aires, Cape Town, Dubai, Los Angeles, Moscow, Shanghai, and Sydney and aim to save their members time, hassle, and money.

In practice

- Such services cost, of course, and may thus be only for those at a senior level or who can persuade their company to budget for it. Nevertheless they deserve a mention here. The time such services can save is considerable and the good operations are well set up. Even when traveling, you can make one phone call in the middle of the night (from a different time zone), arrange to be picked up at the airport, get the dishwasher at home fixed before you get back, and set up a meeting with your bank to explain just why you have been spending so extensively in some obscure foreign currency. Quintessentially has had some exceptional, even oddball, successes: ranging from organizing a visit to the North Pole to see the Northern Lights to having a Premier League soccer player attend the birthday of one member's twin sons for a kick-about.

GIVE YOURSELF SOME TIME RULES

WHEN THINGS GET left, as they can easily do, then it can cause problems, and those problems can waste more time. Something is late. Someone chases. You respond (with excuses?). Moving into firefighting mode, you clear a gap, maybe affecting other matters, and then the omission is made good.

The idea

There is a whole category of things where a simple rule will avoid them being overlooked and causing the sequence of events described above: give yourself an "action now" time rule that prompts to get something out of the way and helps make doing so a habit.

In practice

- You can choose the time extent. You might select two minutes. If something appears needing action and you reckon it can be done in a couple of minutes—do it at once and get it out of the way.

- The time needs to fit your work and activity. For some people it might be two minutes, or ten or something in between, but the assessment you make and how you act because of it can keep what may be a significant percentage of your tasks on the move in a way that prevents them being likely to get delayed or cause problems.

This is an example of a wholly self-imposed discipline, but one that can work well and add to your time management effectiveness just a little more.

30 DON'T WRITE

PAPER CLOGS UP most workplaces—is all your paperwork really necessary? Much of it will be, but some paperwork can be eliminated.

The idea

Resolve always to pause for a second before you write and ask yourself whether what you are about to do is really necessary.

The key alternative to written communication is the telephone; it is usually much quicker to lift the telephone than to write something, and, as not everything needs a written record, this is one of the surest ways of reducing paperwork.

In practice

- It is also worth making a note here about the now ubiquitous email, also an alternative to more formal communication. It is not so much the sense of urgency this bestows on things that interests us in this context (though that is undeniably useful): it is the style. It seems to be that an altogether less formal style has developed for the email. It is one that is perfectly acceptable internally around a big organization with a number of offices, and with people in other organizations, as a quick form of communication where brevity is of the essence. A small point here: email files must be well managed and some must be printed out.

- Two other points are worth a mention. The first is unnecessary copies (a topic dealt with in Idea 26). Second, see if something can be standardized. There may be a number of routine communications that can be retained as standard documents— for example, either whole letters or contracts or separate paragraphs that can be used to put together something suitable. Here technology really does save time. But there is one very important caveat here: never, never use standard material if it is inappropriate. In the sales area, for example, I come across many letters and proposals that shout "standard" when they should be seen as an individual response to the individual customer who receives them. Further, any standard material should be double-checked to ensure that it is well written. Otherwise, by definition, something poor or, at worst, damaging may be sent out hundreds of times a month. It can certainly save time but should not do so at the cost of an unacceptable reduction in quality.

AVOID PURPOSELESS MEETINGS

WHEN DID YOU last lose patience in a meeting? Meetings are held every day without real—or clear—objectives, and take longer and become muddled as a result. And "objectives" does not mean meeting to:

- Start the planning process.
- Discuss cost savings.
- Review training needs.
- Streamline administration.
- Explore time saving measures.

The idea

All meetings should have clear objectives and these should be specific. So saying you will discuss how you might save 10 percent on the advertising budget over the next six months is clear. Better still if that is a figure picked as achievable and it is something currently necessary (despite the effects it might have). At the end of the meeting we should be able to see if what the meeting was convened to achieve has really happened, or is likely to, for such an objective might take more than one short meeting to finalize. More details of this are in Idea 3.

So a specific statement of objectives—which should be in writing in many cases and circulated to all those due to participate—will have a number of effects:

- People will be clear why the meeting is being held.

- They will be better able, and perhaps more inclined, to prepare.

- Discussion will be easier to control, as people will focus more on the topic and the meeting will be more likely to achieve the desired result and to do so in less time than would be the case with a vague description.

In practice

- So, if you ever go to meetings where the objectives do not seem to be clear, ask what they are. Others may well agree that they are not clear, and a few minutes spent early in the meeting clarifying this may be time well spent rather than launching into discussion and finding that the meeting grinds to a halt in confusion half an hour later. Better still, ask before you attend. A clear objective is a real necessity; no meeting without this is likely to conclude its business either promptly or satisfactorily.

HANDLING TELEPHONE INTERRUPTIONS

THE TELEPHONE HAS an insistency that is not easily ignored. Whatever your work pattern, no doubt sometimes you want to be immediately accessible, and on other occasions a task will be completed quicker if you are uninterrupted. Maybe you can get a secretary or assistant to act as a buffer taking calls in the first instance. Clear briefing can rapidly establish those callers you will pause for, those whom to tell you will call back, and those to forget.

This option may not be available, but if you take the call yourself you are at a considerable advantage compared with facing the head round your office door: the caller cannot see you.

The idea

You must resolve to *decide* whether to take calls or not. Some are clearly so important that they override other considerations—in other cases you need to reduce the interruptions. There are certainly people who do not regard saying they are busy, in a meeting, just leaving the office, or similar statements as too much of a white lie if it fends off an unwanted interruption. I even know someone who plays the noise of voices on a dictating machine to give callers the impression that a meeting really is going on! Just like physical interruptions, you can aim to avoid, postpone, or minimize them, and additionally you may wish to devise special responses to particular kinds of call (as below).

In practice

- For example, how many calls do you get from salespeople in a week? Enough for it to be a distraction, most would say. Some of them are useful, some callers you already do business with and you want to maintain the contact. But others you need to get rid of quickly. Most of us are reasonably polite, and we do not like to be rude to people, but consider: only one minute spent on the telephone just to be polite, assuming you spend this with only three telesales people every week, is maybe two and a half hours in a year. And to save this time you still do not need to be rude. Find out at once what they are selling, then you can listen if you want—otherwise a neat sentence really early on will get rid of them fast: "I am sorry, that would not be of interest and I am afraid I am too busy to speak now. Goodbye." Then put the phone down; remember they will aim to prolong the call if you let them. You can always suggest another time to call back if you think a word with them would be useful.

- In all circumstances, people know and understand, from their own experience, that the phone can be intrusive and tend to be more understanding of your not necessarily welcoming a call at a particular moment. So be firm and you will save time.

- All matters of handling these kinds of people interruptions require the normal people-handling skills: tact, diplomacy, but also suitable assertiveness. These need to be deployed in the right mix and to the appropriate degree. If you are seen as insensitive and assertive to the point of rudeness, this may well be destructive of relationships. But if you effectively lie down and ask to be walked on, then it should be no surprise when you are treated like a doormat.

Even more important is the resolve and tenacity that you put into establishing approaches here. Some people—who doubtless work at it—are conspicuously more successful than others at avoiding interruptions. Precedents are easily set, for good or ill. There is a great deal to be gained by getting things right in this area and that includes ensuring you are seen in the right kind of way.

KEEP PAPERS SAFE AND TIDY

I LIKE TO think that I never lose things (well, rarely—let's be honest). But on the last two of those rare occasions, in both cases I discovered the lost paper caught under a paper clip hidden at the back of a batch of other paperwork that was about something quite different. It is a small point perhaps, but you can waste some considerable time hunting for papers and re-collating papers that have got out of order in this sort of way.

The idea

Paper clips are not the best way to keep papers tidy. Beware—they do tend to trap other items and catch you unawares. So save time by banning them and seek another way.

In practice

- To help ensure that your papers are kept tidy, do not keep too much together (it becomes unmanageable), and worry in particular about files and papers that travel about with you both around and out of the office. Staple them, punch them, or bind them rather than use paper clips, and experiment with whatever sort of files—and there are many different styles—suit you. I favor the sort that have a small top and bottom flap to hold things all round and elastic bands that snap across the corners.

- The more things you have to work on in parallel the more your current papers need organizing neatly. If you only get one file out at a time and work on that until it is neatly replaced by something else, then it is less of a problem, but realistically you probably need more around you. If you are paid to keep many balls in the air at once, then this is vital. Time management is, in this respect, similar to juggling. If there are a lot of balls in the air and one is dropped, more tend to follow. The more you have on the go, the greater the disruption and waste of time if something becomes disorganized. Always keep papers physically under control.

DO NOT PUT IT IN WRITING

A TRAINING COURSE delegate once told me that a report he had been asked to prepare had been handed back by the manager to whom he presented it with a request for a verbal summary. While he had lavished care and attention—and thus time—on what was a 20-page report, he was unprepared for this and his spur-of-the-moment presentation was not as fluent as he would have wished. The proposal that the report set out was dropped and the report was never read (it was no doubt filed rather than destroyed). Its writer was naturally aggrieved and resented the incident—with some cause perhaps.

The idea

Certainly management ought to consider the consequences of its action, decisions, and requests to others in time terms. What avoids something taking up time for you may land someone else with a great deal of extra work. If you are a manager, your responsibility for good time utilization covers the team. It is little good being productive yourself if everyone else is tied up with all sorts of unnecessary tasks and paperwork. Jobs need to be done, action taken, consideration given, and in many cases written instructions, guidelines, or confirmation are not simply necessary: they are vital. But on other occasions that may well not be the case. The report referred to above should, in all likelihood, not have been requested. Certainly the action, or lack of it, was decided upon without the detail documented in the report being looked at, and presumably the manager concerned felt he had enough information to make a persuasive case.

This kind of thing can often happen. Time may be wasted unless the instigator of such action thinks first and only specifies whatever action is really necessary.

In practice

- Where does the responsibility for such occurrences lie? It is easy to blame management, but those in receipt of such requests should not be afraid to ask, and check whether such tasks are really necessary. Whichever category of person you are in, and it may well be both, give it a thought.

- Of course, there are other considerations. If you just say, "Shan't" next time the managing director asks for a report, do not come crying to me if you are read the riot act. But in many circumstances a check can and should be made (even with the managing director), and often less paper is put about as a result and time is saved.

35 A MAGIC WORD

EVERYONE HAS TO accept that they cannot do everything. This must probably be taken literally because there may be an almost infinite amount to do, particularly in any job that has some kind of inherent innovative or creative nature to it. Many people could just go on listing more and more things to do, not all equally important, but deserving of a place on their "to do" list nevertheless. Even if your job is not like this, you certainly have to accept that you are not going to do everything at the time you want.

The idea

For reasons of workload and priorities, you are going to have to say "no" to some things. Regularly, and with many people, you need to resolve to think before you agree, and to turn down involvements in some things even though they would be attractive to you (in effect saying "no" to yourself!). Agreeing to things you should turn down will lead you away from priorities; saying "no" is a fundamental time saver. It was well put by Charles Spurgeon: *Learn to say no; it will be more use to you than to be able to read Latin.*

In practice

For instance you may have to turn down:

- *Colleagues*: What is involved here can vary, and if there is a network of favors, with everyone helping everyone else, you do not want to let it get out of hand either way. Turn down too much and you end up losing time because people are reluctant to help you. Do everything unquestioningly and you may be seen as a soft touch and will end up doing more than your share. So balance is the keynote here. Timing is important too; you do not have to do everything you agree to instantly.

- *Subordinates*: Here they cannot tell you to do things, and, though they need support, this must not get out of hand—choose how long you spend with them and ensure the time spent is worth while.

- *Your boss*: Working with a boss who does not have enough to do, or who expects everything to be done instantly just because they are in charge, can play havoc with the best intentions of time management. You may need to regard it as your mission to educate them and have to conduct a campaign of persuasion and negotiation to keep any unreasonable load down.

THE PRODUCTIVE BREATHER

HERE'S A GOOD idea. Time management is about . . . er, productivity . . . and er, well . . . effectiveness. So . . . it . . . that is . . . it's . . .

Sorry, I had to take a break for a moment there. I went to get a cup of tea (very nice too). This took maybe three or four minutes and I do not believe it extended the time taken to put the comments on this topic together; indeed, it helped finalize what exactly to say. After working on any intensive task for a while, most people's concentration flags somewhat; certainly mine does in writing.

The idea

Take a break: an occasional break does not reduce your productivity; it actually helps it. You return to your desk with your head clearer; you feel refreshed and revived by stretching your limbs and can get back to the task in hand with renewed fervor.

This is particularly true of seemingly intractable tasks. Sometimes you can sit and puzzle about things for a long time and appear to get nowhere. After a break it suddenly becomes clear—or at least clearer—and time is saved as a result. Sometimes a break may be as simple as standing up and stretching, or making a cup of tea. Or it may be that something that takes a bit longer is better—you go to lunch even though you originally planned to do that an hour later, or you go for a walk. Once I shared an office with someone who did this—the office was opposite a park and he had a particular circuit that took about ten minutes and provided useful thinking time, perhaps being applied to something else apart from the job from which he had paused. This made a real break, yet was still productive.

In practice

- Recognize that a break is often much more productive than struggling on with a job when concentration is not adequate.

- Alternatively, switch tasks for a moment, rather than stop work, in order to ring the changes.

- A pattern of such activity can become a useful habit if not taken to extremes.

- Something to think about perhaps. Remember what Doug Kling said: *Learn to pause . . . or nothing worth while will catch up with you.* Take a few minutes. It will test the idea.

37 WRITE FASTER

Now "WRITE FASTER" may seem in the same category of advice as maxims such as "Save water, shower with a friend," and you may well ask what you are supposed to do—rush through things so that either you write rubbish or no one can read your writing if you are writing in longhand? Neither—the point I want to make concerns the quality of writing.

The idea

Resolve to write well . . . and quickly. Think of the last reasonably complicated document you had to write, a report perhaps. You had to think about what to say, and designing the structure and sequence of the message and content of this may have taken a little time. Incidentally, you will do this job quicker if you make some notes; it is amazing how many people simply launch into such tasks and then have to redraft what they produce because it becomes a muddle—but I digress. You then had to decide how you would put it. Many people are hesitant in such tasks and find that because they are uncertain of how to phrase things they proceed slowly, with much pause for thought.

Writing is a skill like many others used in business, and it can be improved by study. When my career began to involve me in writing longer and more complicated documents, first reports and proposals, and later books, I started to take an interest in writing style. I read some books, acquired some reference books, and went on a course. I found it interesting (my previous education had had no special bias in this direction) and I found it useful. Some years later, I would still not claim to be the best writer in the world, but I know I write much better than in the past. How to write well and quickly is beyond the brief here, though you might like to check my book *Effective Business Writing* (Kogan Page).

In practice

- The time I spent on improving my writing style was certainly worth while; but I then discovered there was another benefit. I was writing faster. None of this meant that I no longer had to consider what I wrote, and I had not suddenly accelerated out of sight, as it were, but the increase was noticeable and useful; it saved me time. In my work in training I have heard many other people confirming my experience and I have every reason to think that there is a useful potential benefit here, one available to many. Fluent written communication is an important business skill in any case, though one with which many people struggle. If you can learn to improve the standard to which you write *and* gain a bonus in time saved over the rest of your career as well, then some study is well worth while.

38 A COSMIC DANGER

BLACK HOLES, COLLAPSED stars so massive and with such powerful gravity that they pull in everything and even light cannot escape from them, make the old expression about going down the plughole seem pretty small beer. In most offices there are corporate equivalents of this phenomenon, "black hole jobs" that suck in all the time you can think of and a bit more.

The idea

Watch out for such jobs and beware—just like real black holes, if you get too near there is no going back and an involvement means all your other plans have to be put on hold.

What kind of jobs warrant this description? They are usually projects involving a number of different tasks. They are often contentious, may involve an impossibility of pleasing everyone and can be ruinous of reputations, as well as taking up a quite disproportionate amount of time. They include a range of things from arranging the organization's twentieth anniversary party and celebrations to planning the move to new offices. Such things have to be done (you may have such things in your job description, in which case it is a different matter), but they often call for "volunteers." This can mean the managing director suggests it, in public, in a way that makes refusal risky: *It is only a suggestion, of course, but do bear in mind who's making it.* At this point others heave sighs of relief and resolve not to get involved even in a tiny support role.

In practice

- You will know, if you have any wits at all, the kind of tasks in your office that have these characteristics and should, if you value your ability to keep on top of your other tasks, plan to be well away whenever there is a danger of you getting lumbered with one. Do not say you have not been warned.

MORNING, NOON, OR NIGHT

Try as I might, I am not good at working late into the evening, though occasionally this is as necessary for me as for anyone else and I have to make the best of it. On the other hand, I am an early starter and can get on with things effectively comparatively early in the day. I think of myself as a "morning person," know I will get more done in the first half of the day than in the second, and organize myself accordingly—something that affects what I schedule where in the day as much as my actual working practice and productivity.

The idea

Recognize the kind of "time person" you are and organize things, as far as possible, to fit your nature.

There seems to be some scientific basis for this. We do all have rather different biological clocks and it seems to me to be unrealistic to ignore the fact. That is not to say that you can use this principle as an excuse—it is a short step from saying you are at your best in the morning to saying you cannot work effectively after a meal or when there is an R in the month!

In practice

- It is worth deciding what your own personal working pattern is and then working at both accommodating it and overcoming it.

- You may well not be able to work half a day, but you may be able to exercise some choice over when you do what, so that you can place different tasks in different parts of the day in order that those demanding your greatest concentration are tackled at a time when this is most likely to be available.

This is one of many areas where you will never achieve perfection, but that is no reason to ignore it; get things mostly right and you will be more productive and waste less time.

TECHNOLOGY TO THE RESCUE

THE IT REVOLUTION has changed our lives and work practice and continues to do so. Much that can be done is helpful: email is overwhelmingly helpful, not least to time management—though it has its dangers (referred to elsewhere). There is much more, however, and the trick is finding what helps you.

The idea

Resolve to keep an eye on technological developments as they occur, spot and try anything that might help, and adopt anything that can be an ongoing help, making it current practice.

In practice

Any example here will, by definition, probably date quickly. No matter. A couple of current examples make a point.

- Something to check out that you might find useful is the website GoToMeeting.com. This offers a facility to hold remote meetings, coordinating voice communication with the ability for a number of people (only one of whom must be registered with the system) to look at the same thing on the computer screen at the same moment. It is not quite the same as being face to face, but certainly has a role and can save time.

- Another web-based service that is a similar time saver is GoToMyPC.com, which lets you access every detail of your computer remotely; you can literally work on any computer anywhere in the world as if it were your own.

Watch out for such developments; there are almost certainly some that will suit you, and, if there are not now, then there will be.

TIME TO STAY PUT

THOUSANDS OF JOURNEYS must be undertaken every day that are not really necessary. All over the world taxis, cars, trains, and planes are taking people to places to see other people where face-to-face contact is not strictly required. The attendant cost and time cannot even be guessed at. Let us be entirely honest, if a business opportunity presents itself to travel to New York, Singapore, or London, or attend a conference in a well-known resort, then, although overseas and long-distance travel can be very hard work, it can still be extremely tempting. So the first rule in this area is not to accept purely on the basis of your personal pleasure (well, perhaps you can have the occasional treat!).

The idea

Where some form of personal contact is necessary, always consider the alternatives, and resist the reflex that has you rushing away; even a trip from one side of a city to another is time-consuming.

In practice

- Have people come to you: this may be possible, you may only have to suggest it or it may even be worth footing the bill, providing an overnight hotel stay; this will cost no more than you traveling in the reverse direction, and saves you time.

- Send someone else: yes, even to that attractively located conference—delegate.

- Telephone: some things really can be dealt with pretty simply and you do not need to be face to face, or an initial telephone contact gets things started with a visit coming later if necessary (and cellphones increase the options).

- Write or email (remember that with this and the telephone only one produces a record and neither generates such immediate or accurate understanding as a meeting).

- Use technology: for those who are able to afford it, modern telecommunications offers a range of increasingly sophisticated possibilities, including telephone and videoconferencing where you can be linked electronically to a group of people all able to converse and even see each other at the same time, regardless of location.

You do not have to be very numerate to work out how much time could be saved over a year if you cut out even a small proportion of your journeys, one a month, one a week—the hours saved quickly mount up. So before buying a ticket, think for a moment. Of course some things can genuinely only be dealt with face to face and some journeys are essential—but not all.

WHEN BEING REGULAR IS A PROBLEM

HERE IS SOMETHING that occurs in many organizations. There are monthly, weekly, even daily meetings that are held on that particular frequency for no better reason than that they have become a habit. Sometimes, of course, these are necessary, but on other occasions there is nothing, or nothing very much, to discuss and the meeting may then be padded out to make it worth while (it can, in fact, have exactly the opposite effect).

The idea

This practice can lead so easily to time being wasted that it is a good idea to avoid anything having the name "monthly so and so meeting"; it makes it just too easy to keep them going—needed or not.

In practice

- If a meeting is to be held a number of times through the year, consider not just the frequency, but specifically the number and placement of such meetings. For example, maybe you do not need 12 monthly meetings but ten instead, and at some times of the year you need them closer together, while at others (for example holiday times) you can have longer gaps between them. This kind of scheduling will almost always save time.

- It is also good practice to schedule a number of meetings well ahead. So, for the situation referred to above, you would set ten dates for the year ahead, adding a new tenth date at each meeting to keep the future arrangement the same. Everyone knows the problem of getting a group of busy people together at short notice, so this will always work well, particularly if the people involved are disciplined about their diaries and do not allow themselves to be double-booked. Certain meetings are clearly priority occasions and should be regarded as such, remembering that any change disrupts a number of people and thus wastes a disproportionate amount of time.

In this way meetings will be perceived as reflecting their role, rather than any mechanistic formula of, for example, "meeting once a month."

43

TIME TO GET NOTICED

NOT EVERYTHING NEEDS to employ high-tech communication or be passed on instantly; for certain kinds of information old-fashioned methods are still best.

The idea

Use a bulletin board. A strategically placed noticeboard can keep people up to speed on a number of things and creates a place where information can linger for a while (as opposed to the instant deletion possible with an email). It is useful, for example, in giving news of someone's promotion an airing that extends the motivational impact of such an announcement.

In practice

- If your office, or company or department, does not have a bulletin board, get one soon, and then make it clear to people that certain things will not be circulated widely (you can specify the categories of information in advance). A brief notice posted once can save time and it quickly becomes a habit for people to look (though I know one company where they have a "spot the deliberate mistake competition" with a prize to encourage people to look)—worth a try!

THE MOST TIME-SAVING OBJECT IN YOUR OFFICE

ALL SORTS OF things cross your desk: magazines, direct mail, items marked "To read and circulate" and "For information," copies of things that are of no real relevance to you, and minutes of meetings that you wish had never taken place. Much of this pauses for far too long, creating heaps and extra filing trays on your desk and bundles in your briefcase (things to read at home, for instance). It is better to deal with things early rather than later. When they have mounted up, they are always going to be more difficult to get through, and an immediate decision will keep the volume down.

The idea

What is the most time saving object in your office? The WPB. The idea here involves the simple premise of throwing things away. The WPB is, of course, the wastepaper basket. It helps efficiency and time if your desk and office are tidy, if what you need is neatly and accessibly placed—a place for everything and everything in its place—but not if such good order is submerged under sheer quantity of paper, most of it of a "just in case" nature. Clear the clutter and throw unnecessary things away.

In practice

- If you are on a circulation list and do not want to look at something today, then add your name further down the list and pass it on; it will get back to you later when you may be less busy.

- At least check things like a trade magazine at once; maybe you can tear out an article or two and throw the rest away.

- Consider very carefully whether the vast plethora of things that "might be useful" is, in fact, ever likely to be, and either file them or throw them away—regularly.

All such thinking and action help, but most people are conservative and somehow reluctant to throw things away. Unless you are very untypical, there will be things on and around your desk right now that could be thrown out. Have a look, and, as you look, do some throwing. Make a full WPB a target for the end of the day. Imagine it has a scale running down the inside to show how full it is. Such a scale could almost be graduated, not in volume, but in minutes saved.

45 WHAT I MEANT TO SAY . . .

THERE IS A problem with communications that has always existed. It is one compounded by people being busy and that has risen in incidence manyfold since the advent of email. Probably everyone is aware of wasting time with this: you receive an email. It may be from someone you know and about something you recognize, but your first reaction is to scratch your head for a moment and mutter, *What do they mean, exactly?*

Haste and the informal style of email lead to many messages being dashed off. Something is banged out, a click on Send and the sender goes on to something else. What's the result of this? Many messages are ambiguous or completely unclear. Many of the emails criss-crossing the ether are no more than queries. They are sent only to seek clarification on something already received.

The idea

So resolve to slow down a bit. Think about what you write and make sure it will not cause this problem. Does your message make sense? Not just to you, who are in possession of all the facts, but is it likely to make sense to whomever you are sending it to? The alternative—dashing it off—may seem quicker, but in the long term it isn't. You have to write again to clarify; what is more, such an approach risks wasting other people's time and this may well be resented.

In practice

- Think before you write.

- Go on thinking while you type.

- Take a moment to check everything before you click Send (and spell-checking it too is sensible).

- With email, use the Send Later feature, which allows time for second thoughts.

If we all did this, everyone would save some time.

46 AVOIDING MEETING MAYHEM

MEETINGS CAN BE mayhem. No agenda (see Idea 80), no order, confusion and distraction at every turn. Meetings are, or should be, important and, above all, useful. If a "ragged" meeting fails to be constructive, it does no one any good and wastes a considerable amount of time for everyone attending.

The idea

Every meeting must have someone in the chair. More than that, every meeting benefits from a good chair, someone who can lead the meeting, handle the discussion, and generally act to see the objectives of the meeting are met and the agenda is covered in the time allocated. It may be difficult either to take over or to instruct a senior colleague in the art—and it *is* an art—of how to chair a session, but you can at least make sure that any meeting you are to run yourself will be well chaired.

In practice

The benefits of a good chair are considerable:

- The meeting will be better focused on its objectives.

- Discussion can be kept more constructive.

- A thorough review can be assured before decisions are made.

- All sides of an argument can be reflected, and balanced.

- The meeting will be kept more businesslike and less argumentative (even in reviewing contentious issues).

Above all, it will be more likely to run to schedule and achieve the results wanted promptly, efficiently, and without waste of time.

The chairing of a meeting is a skill that must be learned and practiced. It is worth some study. The checklist (Appendix 1 on page 209) will remind you of the essentials, all of which can potentially save time if properly executed.

47 IN THE BEGINNING— OR NOT?

MEETINGS ARE POTENTIALLY time-wasting in a number of different ways. Certainly without some basic organization they can go round in ever-decreasing circles and fail to focus on essentials and get things done.

The idea

Never end a meeting with AOB. Any Other Business, or AOB, is that miscellany of bits and pieces, often the awkward topics, gripes, administrative details, and suchlike, that add tedium and time to a meeting.

Consider what happens if this is taken at the end of the meeting: as the items forming this are tabled—and others are thought of—a long, rambling session can develop that extends the time well past that intended. It also lets the meeting tail away rather than allowing the person leading the meeting to bring it to a firm and, if appropriate, punchy conclusion.

In practice

Taking Any Other Business first and dealing with it promptly should be made a habit—it is a proven time saver.

- First, whoever is in the chair should remind those present what is listed under Any Other Business. This should not include individual items that can be dealt with separately in discussion with just two or three people, and that do not need the whole group present. Any items of this sort should be firmly deferred.

- Then an amount of time should be allocated: *Let's take 15 minutes to get these items cleared up*. With the main part of the meeting still pending, it is much easier to insist that the time specified is adhered to, and that discussion does not become protracted over minor matters. Allowing the latter is a sure way to risk failing to achieve the meeting's main objective, or at least to take longer than necessary to do so.

48 THE CONFLICT/TIME EQUATION

Now LISTEN, PAY attention. It is no good just sitting there lazily scanning the pages, you have to read this properly and . . . Not a good start. Sometimes an approach that is designed to get straight to the point and therefore not waste time has the reverse effect: it rubs people up the wrong way. This ends up producing misunderstanding, dissent, or argument. All of which take time to resolve and the original intention goes out the window. Conflict is not, in fact, entirely bad. It can act as a catalyst to debate, it can help promote creativity and serve to drive for the results necessary in business. But there is a real difference between this and allowing unnecessary conflict to disrupt the smooth running of things and your time being affected along with it.

The idea

I am not suggesting here that the wrong decisions should be made for the sake of a quiet life, but in a number of areas it is a good idea for conflict to be avoided; if unnecessary conflict is absent, then time is surely saved.

In practice

An approach designed to minimize conflict can take many forms, for example:

- In communications: it may be necessary to persuade rather than cajole, and time taken to do so successfully may pay dividends.

- Office politics (of which there is always some) can become intrusive and time-consuming; though ignoring it is dangerous in other ways, it must be kept in its place.

- Personalities can become more important than issues; commercial reason must dictate most of what directs an organization, and untangling personality factors once they have got out of hand takes time.

- Sectional interests also have to be watched.

Operationally, the first step is for consideration of what will be decided, with any discussions, meetings, and everything to do with the process to be kept primarily on a practical basis (there are other issues, of course). If conflict—for instance, about personal issues—is avoided (whether this takes a moment or if complexity means it takes longer), then the time taken to sort something out will almost certainly be less.

49 TOO MANY HEAD CHEFS

WITH THE BUDGETARY pressure on many organizations these days, it is not uncommon for staffing levels to be under pressure too, and one symptom of this may be that organization structure is made to accommodate multiple reporting relationships. This maybe happens in seemingly simple areas, such as when two executives share a secretary or assistant. Or it may be more complex, as with a computer section reporting in part to finance and in part to administration.

The idea

Avoid anyone (especially you!) in any way having two bosses; it is never ideal.

There are likely to be clashes in priorities. Unless there is a clear hierarchy—for instance, with two people sharing a secretary/assistant—there will be problems: whose work gets done first? It could be that an arrangement is fine most of the time, but when it causes problems it tends to cause awkward ones and the likelihood is that something will end up being late. The other example above may pose much more radical clashes: maybe a proposed new program to be used in the computer department suits one of its masters and not the other. Buying two versions might double an already significant cost. Who wins?

In practice

- The one certainty with any situation of this kind is that sorting out the overlaps takes time, actual productivity is reduced, and time is taken up on activity only made necessary by the way things are organized.

- Multi-boss reporting is not usually a good idea. It affects the people involved, and may regularly put them in awkward positions between the two parties.

- Multi-boss reporting also affects other management issues: who appraises the person, who sets their salary, who is actually the overall supervisor? All such things are made more difficult.

So there are a number of good reasons to avoid this situation, and time management that achieves suitable productivity is a key one.

50 AN IDEA THAT GENERATES IDEAS

You HAVE ALL sorts of things to do and all sorts of different kinds of things too—all varying in importance, of course. It is usually true to say that the higher up the hierarchy of an organization you go, the more time you are expected to spend thinking, planning, and decision-making and the less doing other things. It is also often true that any thinking, the planning and idea generation that goes into a job, is usually one of the most important things to be done in that job.

The idea

There is a good training movie on aspects of time management (*Time to Think*). At the end of the movie the main character, a manager who has come to grips with managing his time better, is sitting in his office. A colleague comes into the outer office and begins to walk past the secretary to see him. She stops him, says her manager is busy, and suggests he makes an appointment to see him later. He looks past her at the manager sitting in his office (he is visible through a glass partition) and says: *But he's not doing anything!* Immediately the secretary replies: *He's thinking; now do you want to see him this afternoon or . . .* This incident makes a good point.

What is the most difficult kind of time to keep clear and have sufficient of? Time to think—and think creatively—always ranks high. The moral is clear: one of the most important things your time management practices have to do is to make room for the thinking and creative time your job needs.

In practice

- Consider any analysis of your time you have done, or better still your time log if you have done one (if not you should—see Idea 1), and see how creative activities show up.

- If they are not getting the time they need and deserve or are being squeezed out by other pressures and what seems more obviously urgent, then you need to actively seek a better balance.

- Make sure that you set your sights on sufficient thinking time— perhaps above all—and that the action you take to achieve this is not offset by the crises that all too easily beset any organization or department. Without something approaching the ideal in this area, all your objectives may be in jeopardy.

REWARD YOURSELF

BECAUSE TIME MANAGEMENT is not straightforward—indeed, it requires regular thought—it is easy to take your eyes off the ball and find that your good intentions are not being met.

The idea

If you motivate yourself and give yourself some real reasons to make time management tactics work, you will be more successful at it. Give yourself time management incentives. You need something more than just getting to the bottom of your in-tray. In any case, even the most effective person may never do this, and, while achieving more than expected is perhaps reward enough in some ways, what is wanted is something that is linked more specifically to your own success in managing your time.

In practice

- It thus makes sense to set yourself specific time management goals and to link them to what that will do for you: to give yourself personal satisfaction so that you are very aware that succeeding in what you intend in time terms will make something else possible.

- Such rewards may be seemingly small and personal (they do not have to make much sense to anyone else), but nevertheless an example may make the point. Take my work on this book. I like to have some written work to do when I travel, and an overseas trip tends to contain quite a number of hours that can then be put to good use—on the flight and during otherwise wasted moments. Now the research and planning stage is difficult to do on the move, as I need too many papers and too much space, so if I can complete that and be at the writing stage as I leave on a trip, then this gives me a manageable project to take with me. So completing the initial work in time to fit in with a trip in this way becomes a private goal, and the reward is that I have the right sort of task to accompany me on my travels. This may seem inconsequential, but the point about it is that it is significant to me, and that is what matters.

If you can think in this kind of way and give yourself some sort of reward—better still, a number of them—then your focus on what time management can do for you will be maintained.

BEST TIME FOR APPOINTMENTS

APPOINTMENTS—INTERACTIONS WITH other people—take up a major amount of many executives' time. Many of these occur on a planned basis: they are scheduled appointments.

The idea

Recognize that exactly when you program appointments makes a real difference to your productivity and think carefully about their scheduling. Allow sufficient time; one appointment running into another always causes problems. And always schedule a period of time—in other words, a finishing time as well as a start time. It is impossible to do this with 100 percent accuracy, but it helps to aim for what's ideal.

In practice

Think about:

- The potential for interruptions: an early meeting, before the office switchboard opens, may take less time because there are fewer interruptions.

- The location: where it is geographically makes a difference, and a meeting room may be better than your office, especially if you need to clear the decks and move what you are working on just before it starts.

- Timing that makes it inevitable that it continues into lunch or a drink at the end of the day.

- Timing that restricts your ability to schedule other appointments, in the sense that something mid-morning could mean there is not sufficient time to fit in another meeting before it, or after it and before lunch.

And take especial care with gatherings that involve more than one other person. You have to be accommodating here, but do not always consider others' convenience before your own—it is you who will suffer. Record appointments clearly in the diary and consider separately the various aspects of meetings commented on in a number of other sections.

53 BUT I KNOW WHERE EVERYTHING IS

THERE ARE THOSE who are in no danger of causing a boost to the sales of furniture polish; their desks are totally covered with piles of paper and the wooden surfaces never see the light of day. These are the same people who, if asked about it, always reply, *But I know where everything is*. They mean it too and some of them are right. But, and it is a big but, this kind of disorder rarely goes with good time management. It pays to be neat. This is worth a slight digression. If you are employed by a large organization, you are not indispensable. Sorry, but it is true. What is more, it is incumbent in your responsibilities that you protect the continuity of operations and this includes thinking about what happens if you are, for any reason, not there. Even a short absence by someone on sick leave, say, can cause havoc. It takes others a while to locate things you were working on and thus matters can be disrupted or delayed. Worse perhaps from your point of view, when you return and other people have been rifling through your system, you are not going to be able to find anything.

The idea

So resolve to keep your desk tidy. This means having a clear, and clearly labeled, system, one that is likely to be more specific than an IN and OUT tray and is reasonably intelligible to others.

In practice

- That said, many people like to have things visible. They have a belief that out of sight is out of mind and that this may lead to things being forgotten. Frankly, I share this view. One solution to this is to have a tray (or something bigger if necessary) that contains current project files. I have this to one side of my desk, and the top item in it is a list of those files that are there—because it is a changing population—which helps me check quickly if I am up to date with things. The list, which is in a transparent plastic folder, also records the status of projects and I find this very useful. Thus I believe it is possible to accommodate both views realistically: having key things to hand but keeping your desk clear.

- For most ordinary mortals it is a constant battle to keep things tidy, a battle that ebbs and flows, but one worth keeping a continuous eye on.

ONE THING AT A TIME—TOGETHER

THE DISPARATE NATURE of the tasks most people handle makes managing them difficult. You tend to flit from one to another and need different things in place to tackle each.

The idea

Another overriding principle of good time management is to batch your tasks. Here again proprietary time management systems all have their own methodology, and it is in some cases over-complicated, certainly for my taste, but of course what works best for you is the only measure. I am inclined to believe that more important than the precise configuration of the system here is the number of categories: three to six are ideal simply because that is manageable. It does not matter too much what you call them:

- PRIORITY.

- IMPORTANT.

- ACTION NOW.

- OBTAIN MORE INFORMATION.

- READING.

These are just some of the options (and there are those who manage perfectly well with A, B, and C).

In practice

The key thing is to match the categories to the way you work, for instance:

- You may need FILE and may consider other action categories such as TELEPHONE, DICTATE, WRITE, and DOCUMENT, and similar ones that are particular to your business and your role in it such as PROPOSALS, QUOTATIONS, or the names of products, departments, or systems.

- An important area these days is things that demand you go online. If you have a variety of (genuine) tasks that need you to work in this way, time may well be saved by batching them together.

- A manageable number of batches of this sort can, if you wish, link physically to filing trays on your desk or some distinguishing mark on files themselves. (Incidentally, beware of color coding as the basis for office-wide systems, as a significant proportion of the world's population is colorblind.)

AT THE BOTTOM OF THE PILE

THE NEED TO recognize priorities pervades all thinking about time management. While it is important to identify and deal with key priorities, an inappropriate reordering can occur for the wrong reasons. Things get sidelined for various reasons; here's one deceptively simple one many people fall foul of (and one to be honest about).

The idea

Do not put off the things you do not like.

There is a difference between what you find difficult and what you simply do not like. The likely effect of delay and avoidance of tasks is here very similar to that for things found difficult, but the motivation is different, though nonetheless powerful.

There can be numerous reasons for disliking doing something: it involves something else you do not like, maybe for the best motives (perhaps doing something necessitates a visit to a regional office, which will take up a whole day and involve an awkward journey), or, more often, the dislike is minor—it is just a chore, or a chore compared with other things on your "to do" list. This is perhaps the chief reason why administration is so often in arrears. It is boring and there are other things to do and . . . but you doubtless know the feeling.

In practice

- The only real help here is self-discipline and a conscious effort in planning what you do to make sure that such things do not get left out and that this, in turn, does not lead to worse problems. Some flagging system to highlight things on your "hate" list may act as a psychological prompt; experiment here to see if it makes a difference.

- If all this seems minor and you disbelieve the impact of this area, it is likely that any time log exercise you undertake will confirm the danger. Again it seems simple, but the correct approach can save a worthwhile amount of time.

56

RESOLVE TO "BLITZ THE BITS"

NOTHING IS PERFECT and it is inevitable that as you plan and sort and spend most time on priorities some of the small miscellaneous tasks may mount up. If this is realistically what happens—and for many people it is—then it is no good ignoring it and pretending that it does not occur. Rather, you need to recognize it and decide on a way of dealing with it.

The idea

Make the miscellaneous a priority. Actually, let me rephrase that: make the miscellaneous a priority *occasionally*.

The best way is simply to program an occasional blitz on the bits and pieces. Not because the individual things to do in this category are vital, but because clearing any backlog of this sort will act disproportionately to clear paper from your desk and systems. (Remember 80 percent of the paper that crosses your desk is less important than the rest.)

In practice

- So, just occasionally, clear a few minutes, or an hour if that is what it takes, and go through any outstanding bits and pieces. Write that name in your address book, answer that long outstanding email, phone back those people whom you wish to keep in touch with but who have not qualified recently as priorities to contact, fill in that analysis form from accounts, and do all the other kinds of thing you know tend to get left out and mount up.

- Ideally there should be no bits and pieces. If you operate truly effectively, then this sort of thing will not get left out; it will be dealt with as you go. Really? Pigs might fly. If you are realistic, then, like me, you will find this kind of "catch-up" useful. Be sure it does not happen too often, but when it does, you can take some satisfaction from the fact that a session to "blitz on the bits" clears the decks and puts you back on top of things again. It makes you more able to deal with the key tasks without nagging distractions.

57 "IF I HAD WANTED IT TOMORROW I WOULD HAVE ASKED FOR IT TOMORROW"

PEOPLE CAN BE unreasonable: witness the remark used in the heading here. While many, many things have to be completed by a deadline (including writing this book), it is usually their urgency that causes problems—everything seems to be wanted yesterday (sometimes only because of bad planning) and a cycle of running to keep up ensues.

Deadlines must be addressed realistically. Give yourself sufficient time, build in some contingency, and then you can deal with things properly and still be able to hit a deadline accurately. Fine—or is it? There is another common complication to deadlines: people are dishonest about them. Understandably perhaps—there may be a great deal hanging on hitting one; they affect results and reputations. So what happens is that when something must be done by the end of the month, it is requested for the 25th "to be on the safe side." But this practice, along with the people who do it, becomes known around an office and so the recipient of the deadline assumes that a week later is fine. If several people are involved, then the double-guessing can get worse as misinterpretations are passed on and overall the chances of missing a date increase. It is ironic, but what starts out as a genuine attempt to ensure a deadline is met ends up actually making it less likely that this occurs.

The idea

The moral is clear: be honest about deadlines.

In practice

- In any group with which you are associated, try to make sure the situation about deadlines is clear and open, and that everyone approaches the situation in the same way.

- If something needs completing on the 10th of the month, say so. If some contingency is sensible, say so: *This has to be completed by the 10th. Let's aim to have it ready two days ahead of this to give time for a last check and make sure there is no chance of our failing to keep our promise to them.* Not only does this make it more certain that the deadline involved will be hit, in part because people like the approach and commit to it more wholeheartedly, but it also prevents other things being at risk because time is being spent chasing what is, in fact a fictitious deadline. There is sufficient pressure in most offices without compounding the problem artificially.

58 BE SECURE

WHEN I WRITE the manuscript for a book, I become more and more paranoid as I get a greater and greater proportion of the text written and saved. Every time I do some work on the text, I save it and back it up. At the stage when I have around 50,000 words that might be lost, I do so in triplicate. Well, that's probably exaggerating, but I am very, very careful. These days the hazard for anyone doing work on a computer goes way beyond the machine itself. The things that might cause trouble are legion, and if you spend any time connected to the internet then there is also the risk of viruses, worms, Trojan horses, and more.

The amount of potential damage to work and results, of time spent getting things up and running again if disaster strikes, can be immense. Time is immediately lost, and the more complex the problem the more time will be involved; money too if outside expertise must be called on to right things.

The idea

In light of this snapshot and all that goes with it, the idea here is simple. Keep every aspect of your computer security and management up to date.

In practice

- If you work for an organization of any size, it is likely to have guidelines. Follow them and do so scrupulously. They are there for a reason and there is only one thing worse than having a computer disaster to sort out, and that is having one due to your own negligence. Systems must keep you safe and, if disaster does strike, get your whole system up and running again, not just rescue one part of it or one file. The technicalities in this area change as you watch, so the next two points are in no way comprehensive.

- Back up work, preferably on a hard disk, perhaps also on memory sticks, and do so *regularly*.

- Load and keep up to date the best security software known to man; and check with the experts regularly to see that it remains the best way of fending off everything from spam to viruses.

WHERE YOU ARE MAY BE AS IMPORTANT AS WHAT YOU DO

ENTERTAINING IS REFERRED to elsewhere, but it can take many forms and some of them are a good deal more time-consuming than lunch. Corporate entertaining (and I am not thinking so much of major group occasions such as sponsorship events) can include a wide variety of things from a night at the opera to an evening in a karaoke bar, from a day at the races to an afternoon of golf. Because they involve a very real cost, such things certainly need thinking about, but so too do the time considerations.

The idea

Consider "a day out" in the right way. Take a golf outing as an example. Perhaps a lot of business really is conducted on the golf course; certainly I am not suggesting that such activity is never useful and should be entirely rejected, but its real merits do need assessing. It is not enough that you will enjoy whatever it is, or that the contact will do so. You must ask what will come of it. Will it genuinely move the relationship forward? Is there another way of achieving the same effect with less time expenditure? Can anyone else do it? All these questions need answering. The activity's relevance in terms of time management must be assessed.

In practice

- A golf outing on a Saturday morning, rather than on a weekday, may be a good use of working time, though too many may begin to eat into family time. If three contacts accompany you on one day, then the time may be viewed differently from when there is only one.

- Like so much discussed in this book, just one additional golf outing does not seem vastly significant, but it adds up. Two golf outings a month might use up the equivalent of a whole day, 5 percent of your working time. You need to keep this in mind. Maybe a larger group of people once a month would work equally well.

- Whatever activities of this nature form part of your working life, think about them not as an automatic part of the way things are, something that cannot be changed, but as time that needs to be utilized carefully just like any other. Then you can make the right decisions and know that time is not being wasted.

60 DO A SWAP

Everyone has different skills and also different things they get done most quickly and easily. Some of the things you find laborious a colleague may think to be small beer. You can use this fact to save time.

The idea

As pretty much everyone is in this position, it makes sense to swap some tasks. For example, in sales someone has to analyse, document, and circulate sales results in various forms (to show sales progress, salesmen's targets, results by territory, etc.). If one person is very good at the analysis—crunching the numbers—and another is good at presenting the information graphically—something needing expertise in the right computer program—then perhaps they can collaborate. All the analysis can be done by one, while all the graphic representation is done by the other. The entire job might then be completed more easily and faster—leaving more time to apply to other tasks, primarily dealing with customers.

If such a deal works well, the gain can be considerable. You may want to be on the lookout for suitable swap situations that will help you.

In practice

- Swapping is something that can be done in all sorts of ways around groups of people working together (even in different departments). There is only one possible snag to watch out for and that is any developmental role that is part of a job having been allocated to someone in the first place. If a manager expects you to become familiar with a task and build up some sort of expertise in it, then you are not likely to do that by letting someone else do the work.

- Swap arrangements must turn out to be fairly balanced, of course—if one party finds themselves with far more work than the other, then the arrangement will not last, as someone will end up unhappy. More complex swaps—for example, two smaller tasks for one larger one—may achieve a suitable balance. Choose well and you may evolve a number of such arrangements all around the organization, each of which saves you time. As long as the network does not become too complicated (it must continue to work when you are away for a while, and deadlines must be compatible), then it is one more useful way of saving time on a regular basis.

61 FOOD FOR THOUGHT

FIRST, CONSIDER THE phrase "business lunch." For most people this conjures up something expensive, lengthy, and substantial. If you add in the time taken to get to such an event, then the total time involved is something to be considered very carefully. You need to think about whether to accept such invitations, whether to issue such invitations, and how often to do either. You may need to meet someone, but there may be other ways to achieve this—does it need to be at lunch?

Entertaining is, without a doubt, important. Some contacts (customers, suppliers, and others) don't like it if their goodwill appears to be taken for granted. Yet time is finite and every deal cannot be cemented by a lengthy meal; each occasion should result from a considered decision and be worth while in its own right.

The idea

Make lunch productive. Your contact is, in all probability, as busy as you are. What simple options are there, and what about lunch just for you and colleagues, without customers?

In practice

- Consider simple options for an important contact—for example, can something be arranged in the office? It must be done well, but, that said, it can be good, not take up excessive time, and still meet its objectives. You may well find this option is welcomed by some of your contacts.

- Now let us consider the phrase "working lunch." This is more often internal, and can be very simple—an urgent meeting scheduled for an hour at lunchtime with just coffee and sandwiches provided can make for productivity. Similarly, you may opt to go out for a simple snack with a colleague and do so to discuss a particular thing, often one that has escaped being fitted into your schedule for too long. All this is useful. Sometimes lunchtime needs to be in the nature of a pause, but remember that with around 230 working days in the year, if you took a whole hour at each for lunch, that adds up to more than 25 working days! So it is certainly an area to be thought about extremely carefully.

- A final, cautionary, note: watch what you drink at lunchtime. Alcohol may help the atmosphere during lunch, but too much is not going to help you maintain or improve productivity in the afternoon. I wonder how often when someone is described as "not back from lunch" it really means they are asleep at their desk.

LESS IN TOUCH, MORE TIME

MANAGEMENT, ESPECIALLY SENIOR management, can very often become protected and cloistered to the point that it has no genuine feel for how other parts of the organization work. This can waste time when a problem or opportunity arises and research needs doing before whatever it is makes sense.

The idea

The idea here is to ensure that you see and talk to your people regularly and directly. Like so much else, how and when this is organized should be to a conscious plan: one conditioned not least by the time that will be taken up. How do you approach this? This has become a technique in its own right, with its own abbreviation: MBWA—Management By Walking About. However good the management control systems that exist in an organization are, there is no substitute for you going and seeing and hearing first hand what is going on, what the problems are, and what opportunities are present.

In practice

- MBWA is a real aid to communication, and it can also save time. At its most dramatic, one fact-finding walkabout can negate the need for several meetings and a report, as the evidence of your own eyes and ears jumps you ahead in the decision-making process. Getting this first-hand input makes a real difference to your ability to operate, so the balance of time here—taken and saved—is likely to be productive. This is especially true if you can find ways of creating opportunities for this that serve more than one purpose.

- A good example of this occurred when I was conducting a course. The client's managing director both introduced the program and returned to round things off at the end. Apart from it being good practice for senior management to support a training culture, this was classic MBWA. Drinks were available and the managing director regularly interrupted his discussion with his people to make notes—matters identified for later follow-up. This can happen quite naturally as the chat mixes with more serious comment. The point, made clear to me later, was that he consciously saw such a gathering as serving a double purpose: he was happy to support training, but more ready to do so if it provided an opportunity for some of the "walking about" he felt necessary.

IN TIMES OF (TRAVEL) TROUBLE

BUSINESS TRAVEL DOES not always go smoothly. This is an area where we all hope nothing will need doing, but if there is any sort of emergency—an accident, illness, or crime—then there is every reason to be prepared in advance. And one of those reasons is to avoid the substantial amount of time that may be wasted in sorting things out otherwise.

The idea

The premise is simple: assume there will be problems and organize for them. A little time spent up front can save a great deal of difficulty later that would take much longer to sort out (and perhaps in trying circumstances too).

In practice

- The first piece of advice is simple enough. Never travel abroad unless you are insured. Now, you may think, *No problem, the organization will sort it,* but do you know how? If something occurs, do you have to telephone the office even to be reminded of the name of the insurance company, or can you immediately make contact with someone local who will help? It is worth checking (if you are in a different time zone it may be hours before your office is open).

- The second is a simple and wise precaution. Imagine one of the worst scenarios: you are overseas and you lose your wallet or briefcase. What do you have to do? It is quite a list: advise your credit card companies (it is often more than one), sort out a new passport, get more traveler's checks, confirm flights for which you now have no tickets (not even e-tickets), get enough money fast enough not to have to walk to your next meeting and beg for a free lunch from your appointment. There could be more, your wallet may have contained telephone numbers or addresses, for instance, that need replacing. Much of the arranging you cannot avoid, but if you leave a record in your office of all the key things—credit card numbers, traveler's checks, air tickets, etc.—then an email saying as little as "wallet lost" means someone can get working on your behalf and you can go off to your next meeting without pausing to worry about some of the items at all.

- Of course, such items can be in a hotel safe some of the time and that's worth making a habit too. Let us hope that you never get into this kind of situation, but if you do—be prepared.

64 WHILE YOU WERE AWAY

WITHOUT A DOUBT a vast amount of time must be wasted in offices around the world because of inaccurate or incomplete messages. Time is wasted wondering what things are about, with things said once being repeated and other things having to be rectified or reiterated because of errors or breakdowns in communication.

For most people there are bound to be times when you are away from the office, even if such absences are brief or infrequent.

The idea

A good message system in your office will save you time and prevent any misunderstandings causing problems. You need a message form that is designed for you. The information you want may not be exactly that on the forms that commercial stationery companies sell. In this way *your* form acts as a checklist for those around the office as to the information you want noted.

In practice

- If such forms are in a style that declares their importance—after all, one lost message may change history (or at least cause major corporate or personal inconvenience)—they can save more time. You must decide what suits. Maybe a full-size (A4) page is best (it means it can clip together with other papers to make a neat file as well as being more visible); maybe it should be on colored paper so that it stands out among other office paperwork.

- Small differences here are important. For example, a section for ACTION TAKEN as well as ACTION REQUIRED tells you exactly how far a conversation proceeded and allows follow-up without repetition. You might start with a standard form, but do not copy it—adapt it.

- So decide how a system should work for you, how messages should be taken, and when, where, and how they should be passed on.

"WELL, IT'S ALWAYS BEEN DONE LIKE THIS"

YOU MAY WELL deny, if asked, that you spend time doing things that are unnecessary; after all, it seems absurd. But it does happen. And it happens for all sorts of reasons. Consider a few examples:

- *Habit*: You have always attended a monthly meeting, read a regularly circulated report, checked certain information, filed certain items, and kept in touch with certain people. And it is easy for things to run on, repeating automatically without thought, and for such things to take up time unnecessarily.

- *Insurance*: You do things for protective reasons. In case something goes wrong, in case someone asks why, in case . . . what? Sometimes the reason is not clear; there is just a feeling that it is safer to do something than not.

- *Expectation*: You do things not because of their real worth, but because they are, or you feel they are, expected of you. In a team environment you do not want to let others down, though you will let them down more by ignoring priorities.

- *Appearances*: You do things because they are "good things" to be involved with, perhaps politically, and every organization has some politics. Your position and perception around the organization are important, but you must not overdo this kind of involvement, not least because it can become self-defeating, with people seeing it as an ego trip by someone who has nothing better to do.

The idea

This is an area to address very hard. Are there any things you are doing that you can stop doing without affecting results significantly? For most people an honest appraisal shows the answer to be "yes," so such a review both immediately if you have not done one for a time, and regularly to ensure that unnecessary tasks are not creeping in again, is very worth while.

In practice

- How is this done? Very simply—you ask why? Why is something being done? And if the answer is because that is the way it is, that is the system, or, worst of all, that is the way it has always been done, then ask again. If you can really not find a better reason, then the task may well be a candidate for elimination. Failing that, maybe you can do it less often, in less detail, or otherwise adjust the approach to save time and divert attention to the priorities.

66 I WAS JUST PASSING

An organization is a club, colleagues are acquaintances or friends, and work can be fun, and this can make for problems as when, for example, "Good morning" turns into half the morning disappearing in chatter.

Now I am not suggesting that all social contact is forbidden, perish the thought. I like a chat and some gossip as much as anyone; indeed, without some of this to foster relationships, an organization would be not only a duller place but a less effective one. There is an indefinable dividing line between the social chat and the business content, and curtailing anything we cannot definitely label "business" will risk throwing the baby out with the bath water.

The idea

On the other hand, you do need to keep things in proportion. So resolve to curtail excesses and watch out for those moments at which the danger that time will be really wasted is greatest.

In practice

Dangerous times include:

- First thing in the morning, when greetings tend to turn into an in-depth analysis of the meal, date, TV show or movie, sporting event, or disaster of the previous evening.

- Breaks, when the coffee comes round or people gather around the drinks machine.

- Lunch, when even the process of discussing when to go, with whom, and where can assume time-consuming proportions.

- The end of the day, when everyone is getting tired and a chat is a welcome excuse to wind down early.

There are places too where you are prone to get caught and conversation runs on. In some companies, the reception area acts as a sort of plaza with people passing through it in different directions using their chance encounters as an excuse for a chat. Every office layout has its own version of this.

Because people's work patterns are different, and because you can benefit from the occasional break (see Idea 36), moments when you have time for a chat may not suit others and vice versa. If everyone thinks about this in a constructive way, then some—necessary—chat will occur, but in the context of mutual respect for people's time and without what you intended to be a two-minute pause turning into half an hour and two cups of coffee. So beware and be careful—there is no need to be standoffish and there is particularly no need to screen out useful conversations, but remember that this can be a major factor eating away at productivity, and act accordingly.

ENCOURAGE AND HELP OTHERS

PEOPLE WHO WORK together in an office can be infected by the prevailing practices and habits. In an office where some people habitually arrive late in the morning and nothing is said, more people will tend to follow suit and the situation will spread and get worse. This is a negative point, but the principle is the same with the positive.

The idea

If you want time management to be an issue that people care about, think about, and work at, then you must take the initiative and lead by example.

In practice

Several practices may be useful here, for example:

- *Set up standard systems*: It is not too dictatorial to set up, and insist on, certain systems that you feel will help everyone's time utilization: for example, the same priority codes used around the office, the same basis for completing diaries (or even the same diary or time system), an insistence on tidy desks—and more.

- *Use standard reporting procedures*: Here again a standard helps. Such things as memo style, when, where, and how meetings are scheduled, bulletin boards, all can help create a climate of efficiency if they are well organized.

- *Explain*: If you tell people why you do certain things, work in certain ways, and why you expect them to do likewise, then it is more likely that, seeing a good and personally useful reason, they will comply.

Once practice in these things occurs, habits follow and then the time saving around and among a group of people accumulates. So be a public advocate for the virtues of time management, say you believe in it, say you practice it, and do not just expect your team to follow suit—make it easy for them by introducing them to the systems and laying down a few rules to make it all stick. If you help them in these kinds of ways, it will help you too.

TO MEET OR NOT TO MEET . . .

How OFTEN HAVE you come out of a meeting and not only been dissatisfied but wondered what you were doing there or even why the meeting had been held at all? If you answer "never," then you must work for an extraordinary organization, and if it is "often" you are in good company.

The idea

The idea here is simple—avoid unnecessary meetings. That said, there are two situations we must consider here: your meetings and others to which you are invited.

In practice

Consider two kinds of meeting:

- *Your meetings*: Before you open your mouth to say, "Let's schedule a meeting," pause, think—and think of the alternatives. Ask questions: is the proposed topic a matter for debate or consultation, or can you make a decision without that? Can any information that will be disseminated at the meeting be circulated any other way? If brief conversation is necessary, is it enough to have a word on the telephone, in the corridor, or over a working lunch? Often the answer suggests an alternative, and a briefer one than a meeting. If so, make a telephone call, send a note, or take whatever action may be called for to achieve what you want. Remember to consider the time spent by everyone at the meeting. It is right to think of six people meeting for an hour as representing the equivalent of six hours' work: more, in fact, because people have to prepare, to get there—and someone must set up all the arrangements. It is an important part of any meeting convener's responsibility to think carefully about who should attend, remembering that every time another name is added to the list, not only will this take up that person's time but it will extend the duration of the meeting.

- *Others' meetings*: With these, while there will be some you must attend, the same applies: think first before you agree to participate. You may find there are things you attend for the wrong reasons (just to keep in touch, or just in case something important crops up, perhaps). Maybe the minutes are sufficient to accommodate this. Or maybe, if you are a manager, it is important for your section to be represented, but you can delegate someone else to attend and report back to you. This may take some resolve. There may be aspects of the meeting you enjoy, topics on which your contribution allows you to shine, but it may still not be a priority to attend.

In either case, whatever the meeting is about, make sure it is essential, and that there is no alternative.

CATEGORIZE TO MAINTAIN THE BALANCE

FEW PEOPLE ARE bad time managers because they are idle. Certainly most of those with an interest in time management are busy people, but they may not be getting everything done, or everything done thoroughly and on time. And the thing that gets neglected most is investment time, time taken now to ensure improvements or results in future—the planning and analysis and other such activities necessary to make progress in any area.

The idea

Categorizing on your plan which sort of time you are scheduling will help create a balance (it has been mentioned elsewhere that diary and "to do" lists should schedule tasks—and some people evolve a code to differentiate between various sorts of task in this way). Thus the plan will show whether time is to be taken up with people (appointments, meetings, etc.) or tasks (and whether they are action or investment oriented), and will allow for the unexpected.

In practice

- You should be able to be see at a glance, maybe in the double opening of a loose-leaf book, what falls into which category so that fine-tuning can take place if necessary. After all, time planning should be a guide and assist you in the way you work, not act as a straitjacket that restricts you.

- If you have a good feel for how much of your job should be spent in action time and how much in investment time, then you will be better able to create and maintain the balance you need, using the techniques of time management to create the working pattern you want. Time management is, and should be regarded as, a personal tool, something that you use to help you and not a standard approach that you must adopt just in order to be efficient in some academic sense.

ON OCCASION, LET'S TALK

THINGS EASILY FALL into a pattern and become a habit. This can happen without conscious thought and thus bad habits can build up as easily as good ones. Any development in the way things are done can promote change, and one thing that has revolutionized the world of work in recent years is email. Email is quick and easy, and you are entitled to wonder, as I do, how you could manage without it. But it can take over. It can become such a reflex to click on "Write a message" or "Reply" that people cease to talk to each other.

As a result, some organizations have rules—for example, forbidding people to send any internal emails on, say, a Wednesday.

The idea

Just remember that it is often better to talk to people and maintain a proportion of your communication as face to face or, failing that, telephone contact rather than something more distant and impersonal.

In practice

- Follow any rules like that mentioned above, especially when people are nearby (people regularly email others working in the same room!).

- Consider the nature of the communication. Is it something demanding explanation (and thus needing care to put in writing, which will take time)? Is it to be persuasive and thus better done face to face? Should it carry motivational overtones (as from a manager to a staff member)? There are many different reasons for favoring communication in forms other than writing.

- And consider the time implications. It may take a minute or two more to get up and go to someone, but if it is more likely to create accurate communication or achieve more, then it may well save time in the end, as well as being more pleasant.

71 WELL SPOTTED

At the dawn of the computer revolution we were promised "the paperless office." For most people there is still plenty about. What's more, if it is disorganized it causes problems: things get lost, and time is wasted. A particular problem is the number of times the same pieces of paper can cross the desk; every crossing uses up some time.

The idea

So you need to reduce the number of times you see and deal with the same piece of paper. For example, a letter arrives today and you read it (1), you decide not to deal with it immediately but put it with a job on which you intend to spend time in the afternoon (2). In the afternoon you make a start, work out what needs to be done but are interrupted (3). The letter joins a number of items that overlap the day and you pick it up again the following morning (4). And so it goes on, even with a simple letter. In other cases matters may span weeks or months. To reduce multiple handling you need to make the problem tangible.

Here is an easy experiment you can try. Select, say, ten items arriving on your desk today—a mixture of letters and documents all of which demand some action on your part—and mark them all with a red spot in the top right-hand corner. Then simply deal with them as normal. And every time you touch them thereafter add another red spot to the top right-hand corner. As time passes you will then produce a count of how many times things go through your hands.

This is known as the "measles test." It can help you identify how your way of handling things affects the time taken. Sometimes the multiple "spotting" is necessary, but in other cases the number of spots will surprise or appal you.

In practice

The first step in introducing change is to know where change should be applied, and it is this that the measles test shows you. So:

- If you have a clear plan and a system for categorizing your work, then things should be dealt with immediately, or held for some reason and then dealt with. If this is done rigorously, then the time taken up by papers being handled many times will be reduced.

- You need sufficient sight of some items to operate effectively and must be careful not to reduce paper handling inappropriately. However, the principle advocated here is sound, and as a general rule being aware of how many times things go through your hands and trying to keep that number down makes good sense in time terms.

72 FIGHTING THE PLAGUE

SPAM IS A modern electronic plague. One newspaper reported someone getting 44,000 junk emails every day (16 million a year!). For most of us, therefore, it could be worse, but it is a problem, and dealing with it is estimated to cost every computer user several hundred pounds each year in lost time. The numbers rack up largely because of "zombie computers": those infected by spammers and persuaded to send out spam emails without their owner's knowledge. There are reckoned to be more than 10 million of these in Britain alone. Though Bill Gates said in 2004 that spam would be gone within two years, the problem just seems to get worse and worse and normal precautions may not be sufficient.

The idea

In addition to setting up standard spam filters, which shunt incoming spam into a separate inbox, consider using a more specialist anti-spam software such as ClearMyMail; even though there is a small subscription cost for such services, such action can prove worth while. Nothing dates quicker than anything to do with computers, so readers may need to check out the best of such services at the time they think about using one.

In practice

* The things to be careful of here are to keep whatever solution you go for up to date and, in an organization of any size, to double-check that you only take action in a way that sits comfortably with the policy and practice of the organization and any rules an IT department may lay down.

73 LET THE PLANT GROW

CONCENTRATING ON PRIORITIES is a key factor in good time management. These need deciding, and also in the light of changing circumstances they may need ongoing review and adjustment.

That said, some people use up hours of valuable time thereafter reviewing their decisions again and again to double-check them. In effect it is like digging up a plant to look at the roots to see if it is growing well. Some people seem to seek constant reassurance about their decisions, and this can just waste time and is also, in my view, a certain route to stress.

The idea

Trust your decisions about priorities. Having considered their selection thoroughly, you make a decision. There is no reason at that point to doubt that it is other than a good one. And, in any case, no amount of further review will change the fact that you can do only one thing at a time, and, however illogical, it is this that a long list of things to do sometimes prompts us to look to change. It does not matter whether the first thing to be done is followed on the list by ten more or a hundred more: something has to be done first. Action must follow.

So make the decision, stick to it, and get on with the task. The quicker you do that, the sooner you will be able to move on down the list.

In practice

Stress is seemingly a common problem, yet stress is a reaction to circumstances rather than the circumstances themselves. You should be able to say that you:

- Know your priorities.
- Have made work-planning decisions sensibly, basing them on reasonable and thorough consideration of all the facts.
- Are sure there is no more, for the moment, you can do to make things easier.

Knowing you have made good decisions, and are now proceeding to implement them, should allow you to be comfortable about the process, and to reject any tendency to stress. Just worrying about things, and worrying at them, when you should be getting on and taking action is a sure recipe for stress. Keep calm by keeping organized and you will be better placed to maintain and increase your effectiveness.

74 OVER TO YOU

For managers, if a task must be done, but you cannot get to it, then the best way to give yourself more time is to delegate it to someone else. This is eminently desirable and yet, for some, curiously difficult.

So let's look at the difficulties. Delegating is a risk. Something may go wrong and, what is more, as the manager, you may be blamed. So, despite the fact that the risk can be minimized, there is temptation to hang on to things. This makes for two problems: you have too much to do (particularly too many routine tasks) and this keeps you from giving due attention to things that are clear priorities. And staff members do not like it, so motivation—and productivity on the things they are doing—will also be adversely affected.

An additional fear is not that the other person will not be able to cope, but that they will cope too well—being better than you. But this is not a reason that should put you off delegating—the potential rewards are too great. Besides, people are more likely to do things differently and that can help development of both individuals and methods.

The idea

So don't do it—delegate.

The amount you can do if you delegate successfully is way beyond the improvement in productivity you can hope to achieve in any other way. All that is necessary to make delegation successful is a considered and systematic approach to the process such as that detailed in Appendix 2.

In practice

What does successful delegation achieve? There are five key results:

- It creates opportunity for development and accelerated experience for those to whom matters are delegated.

- It builds morale (precisely because of the opportunity noted above) through the motivational effect of greater job satisfaction, and achievement long and short term in the job (and ultimately beyond it).

- It has broader motivational effects around a team, as well as on the individual.

In addition, there are advantages to you. As a result of the time freed up:

- Time and effort can be concentrated on those aspects of your job that are key to the achievement of objectives.

- A more considered, or creative, approach can be brought to bear, uncluttered by matters that may distract or prevent a broad-brush or longer-term perspective.

75 KNOW WHEN TO LEAVE WELL ALONE

SOMEONE MANAGING A team has to give members of that team space to complete the tasks they are engaged in, whether these are work that simply has been allocated or jobs that have been delegated. There is a temptation, perhaps particularly when a job is first delegated and you worry whether it will be done right, not only to check up but to do so on a frequent and ad hoc basis. Because this is offputting to those who may be at some midpoint on a job—a point at which things are not finished and look that way—it can actually end up delaying completion and perhaps giving you a false impression of their capabilities. Checking up takes time and may set back the way things are going rather than help. Certainly too overt an approach does nothing for motivation.

The idea

Do not hover. If something needs checking, and it may well do, then such checks should be discussed and agreed at the start of the work. Then the people concerned know what to expect. They can plan for any checks at particular—known—moments, and such checks will, as a result, be more likely to be constructive—or, indeed, unnecessary, as those concerned will work to make sure that when the monitoring process arrives all will be on schedule.

In practice

- If you work to make such checks an agreed part of the plan, if you make them constructive, then you will not have to spend very much time on them at all. The team working well, with minimal supervision, is a great asset to any manager wanting to conserve their own time.

- A manager who hovers unnecessarily is resented, and any resulting element of poor relations with staff tends to be time-consuming.

IS THAT THE TIME?

Anyone who travels long haul will know it is tiring, cramped, uncomfortable, and dehydrating. They are apt to serve you two dinners in quick succession when it is lunchtime and wake you up when you want to sleep. Getting out of economy, if you can afford it, will make you somewhat more comfortable, but it will not lessen the effect of jet lag. If you get off the plane feeling like death, and there are other distinct effects such as an inability to concentrate as well as normal, then it is not advisable to go straight into the most important meeting of your trip.

The idea

Resolve to work at minimizing jet lag (to some degree). Doing so will mean you are more productive and more effective more quickly after a long-haul flight, something that could save a whole day as well as result in better action.

So what's the answer? Can you cure it? The short answer is "no"; the only remedy is time. But there are things you can do to minimize the effect, starting with picking a flight that arrives at a time that suits you. This really is a very individual area and everyone has their own way of dealing with the experience, from just giving up on it and drinking too much (someone like this always seems to sit next to me) to dubious potions and concoctions of vitamins. Some of the time on the flight you may well be able to use constructively, a thought reviewed separately, and on arrival you may want to schedule a few simple tasks that do not demand any real concentration. Beyond that you can experiment and see what suits your constitution and seems to help.

In practice

I regularly make several long-haul return trips each year: certainly enough to have made me think about it. So I record here what I do in case this fits for you:

- I never drink alcohol (this is every doctor's advice).

- I drink more than I think I need to (to combat dehydration).

- I never eat more than the smallest snack (this will not suit everyone, but jet lag is partly digestive and I find arriving hungry and eating the right meal going by local time definitely helps).

- I sleep at the time that applies in my destination (I help this by adjusting bedtime on the night before flying and taking a sleeping pill during the journey).

Anyway, this helps me. You will do well to think about how you react and what can help you, as jet lag is a certain time-waster, and, worse, you can find it affecting your performance as concentration is impaired. Experiment and see if you can make a difference here.

77 MAKING IT CLEAR

TOO OFTEN MANAGERS find themselves in a crisis to which the resolution would be all too easy if they could wind the clock back. "If only we had done so and so earlier," they say contemplating a messy and time-consuming process of unscrambling. Realistically, though the unexpected can happen sometimes, crisis management is all too common, and often all too unnecessary. Coping well with crises that are, for whatever reason, upon us saves time—certainly if the alternative is panic.

If things are left late or ill thought out (and the two can often go together), then time is used up in a hasty attempt to put things right at short notice. This tends to make any task more difficult and is compounded by whatever day-to-day responsibilities are current at the time.

The idea

If you can acquire the habit of thinking ahead, and a system can help you do this, then you are that much more likely to see when action really needs to be taken on something. This might appropriately be called the opposite of the "if only . . ." school of ineffective time management.

In practice

- Some people find that to "see" the pattern of future work and tasks in their mind's eye is difficult. One invaluable aid to this is the planning or wall chart (also mentioned in Idea 23). This enables you to create a picture of activities, and the time spans are very much clearer as you scan such a chart than when flicking through the pages of a diary.

- Charts come in all shapes and sizes; some are for the current year and are, effectively, large diaries, others are ruled for specific tasks, and others still are designed for you to create the detail. The large ones come with a variety of stickers to help highlight what is important; some are even magnetic and can provide a permanently updatable guide to your schedule.

- Whatever you do to document things, however, the key is to get into the habit of thinking ahead—as you deal with things, but without disrupting the current day's workload. Anticipating problems and spotting opportunities can make a real difference to the way you work in the short term.

78 SOLDIERING ON

THERE IS AN important but simply stated point to be made here about health, something that can all too easily be neglected because of pressure of work. Long-term health is one thing (and beyond our scope here—except to say that reducing pressure should avoid ongoing stress in the negative sense), but your day-to-day state of health has some essentially practical implications. Deadlines and the projects that have them are important. But no one is indispensable (it may be a sobering thought, but it is true). If you were not there, then other arrangements would have to be made; a few, perhaps lesser, priorities might suffer, but things would for the most part work out. Yet, if illness threatens (and I mean minor illnesses rather than being rushed into hospital), there is a great temptation to struggle on, and this tendency is more pronounced when an important deadline is looming.

The idea

Don't soldier on regardless. Now I am not suggesting that you take to your bed at the first sign of every tiny sniffle, but this is worth thinking about logically in a way that balances short- and long-term considerations and the time implications of both.

In practice

- If a couple of days struggling on ends with you being away from the office for a week once you have to give in to whatever bug you may have picked up, and a day off right at the beginning would have caught the thing in the bud, then this is not the most time-effective way of dealing with it.

- Obviously, it may be difficult to predict the course of minor ailments, but it is worth a moment's thought, and certainly it is often the case that the instant "I am invaluable and must struggle on" response is not always best. Quite apart from anything else, you do not want to sneeze all over everyone for several days, then take to your bed and, on your return, find that the whole department has caught the bug from you so that everyone is off sick and the impact on time has escalated.

DRIVEN TO DISTRACTIONS

IN THE AGE of the sound bite, it is becoming increasingly difficult to concentrate on anything for five minutes; what is more, we are all in danger of not only trying to do more than one thing at a time but believing we can. This is most evident in working on the computer; indeed, the system and the ability to have different things on screen at the same time compound the situation. We go to send an email and find ourselves answering another, deleting spam, and trying to take an incoming phone call all at the same time, while talking to a colleague standing by our desk and holding open with one hand a document we need to consult. It. Does. Not. Work.

The idea

The idea is simply to concentrate on one thing at a time. And the logic of so doing is especially powerful when the tasks involve language—as, of course, both emailing and speaking, on the telephone or otherwise, do.

In practice

- Psychological studies are now showing more and more clearly that if a good job is to be done attention must be focused. Particularly, the language channels in the brain cannot cope with doing two things at once. Write an email while talking on the telephone and one or other, or even both, will suffer—and sorting out any difficulties created will waste time.

- If you doubt this, try reading the book *Distracted: The Erosion of Attention and the Coming Dark Age* by Maggie Jackson. It presents some seriously scary thoughts about the consequences of shrinking attention spans (and it might also make you think twice before using a cellphone, even a hands-free one, in your car ever again—time in A&E is hardly likely to improve productivity).

- As the irresistible march of technology adds more and more complexity to our lives, this is certainly something to keep an eye on; if it causes difficulties now, what will it be like in five years and how much time will we then waste unless we moderate our unthinking belief that we can do it all at once?

A CLEAR AGENDA =
A SHORTER MEETING

MANY MEETINGS ARE run without an agenda (Latin for "things that must be done"), and this can be the cause of confusion and thus wasted time.

The idea

Resolve to draw up a written agenda and, for many meetings, to circulate it in advance. It need not be elaborate, but you should always have one. You should check the overall look and balance of the agenda to make sure that too much is not being attempted in the time available. If patience runs out, things will end up taking longer or will not have justice done to them. And, perhaps above all, the agenda should reflect the objectives set for the meeting; indeed, although a conventional agenda item does not usually state why something is being discussed, you may find that a longer version is useful and actually serves to speed up the meeting.

In practice

The agenda should do a number of things:

- Specify the formalities (do you need to note apologies for absence, for example?).

- Pick up and link points from any previous meetings to ensure continuity.

- Give people an advance opportunity to input to the meeting content, if this is required.

- Specify who will lead or contribute in any particular way to each item, in part to facilitate preparation.

- Order the items for discussion or review. This is something that may need to represent the logical order of the topics, the degree of difficulty they pose (and perhaps the time they will take), the participants' convenience (maybe someone has to leave early and you want an item to be dealt with while they are still present).

- Reflect any "hidden" agenda; for example, with a controversial issue being placed to minimize discussion (perhaps just before lunch).

- Deal with administrative matters such as where and when the meeting will be held, and, if it is long, whether appropriate refreshments will be served.

THE MOST TIME SAVING PHRASE IN THE ENGLISH LANGUAGE

FOR ANY MANAGER this may be the most important section in this book. There is a scene that is played out in offices all over the world and must waste untold hours every single day. Imagine a manager is busy at their desk when a head comes round the door and a member of staff comes in. "What is it?" the manager asks. And the reply is something like: "I'm not sure how to handle so and so and wondered if you would just check it with me." The manager thinks for a second—busy, in the middle of a job, and not wanting to lose concentration—but the interruption has already occurred. So their first thought is to minimize the interruption and get back to work fast. Thus, if the matter allows, they spend a minute or two explaining what to do and then tell the other person to let them get on and the brief impromptu meeting is over. This may be done kindly or abruptly—the effect is much the same—and the scene may be played out repeatedly for an individual manager.

But suppose the same manager is away from the office for a couple of days. While they are away, people will face similar situations. If the manager was there, they would go and ask. Because that's not possible, they simply get on with the job, they make a decision, they take action, and life goes on. When the manager returns to the office, what do they find? A chain of disasters? A plethora of wrong decisions and misjudged actions? Rarely is this the case. The things that might have been checked have been done, and not only is no harm done—everything has probably gone perfectly well.

Think about it. I suspect this scenario will ring bells with many, if not most, managers. Why does it happen? It is a classic case of thinking that it is quicker to do things for people, most often in this instance providing the answer or the decision, rather than to take any other action. I believe this is wrong.

The idea

You have to take a longer-term view, and this is where the most time saving phrase in the language comes in. Next time you are interrupted in the way I have described, try responding by saying: *What do you think you should do?* They may not know, but you can press the point, prompt them to make some suggestions, and, when they do, then ask which solution they think is best. This takes a few minutes, certainly longer than the response described earlier, but if they are coping when you are not there to ask, then you will find that when you prompt them they most often come up with a good answer (there is rarely any one right way). At that point you can say something like "That's fine," and away they go to carry on, leaving you to get back to your own work.

In practice

* Now this is not just a better way of dealing with this situation—indeed, at this stage, you may say it is worse as it prolongs the interruption. But it is doing something else of very real value: it is teaching your people not to interrupt, but rather to have the confidence to think matters through unaided. You have to be insistent about this. It will not work if you only make people think it through when you have more time, and still provide a quick answer when you are busy. Every time—every single time—someone comes through the door with a question about

something with which you believe they should be able to deal unaided, you say: "What do you think you should do?" It must become a catchphrase. And, as this practice continues, the message will get home to people, so that if they even start to think of asking you they can hear your likely response in their mind. You will find such questions coming less and less often. You will also find that, if they do ask, people move straight to the second stage, and come in with two or three thought-out options just wanting you to say which is best. Resist. Ask them. The message will stick and, surprise, surprise, you will find you are saving time. What is more, your people will almost certainly get to like it more also, especially if you comment favorably on how well they are doing on the decisions they are making unaided.

- All this needs is some persistence and determination. Early on you may think it is taking too much time, but the investment formula will surely pay off. There are considerable amounts of time to be saved here, linked directly to the number of people who report to you. Do not be faint-hearted about this; it is very easy to break your resolve in a busy moment and send someone on their way with an instant dictated solution. Exceptions to your consistency will just make the lesson take longer to get over. But this idea really does work in the longer term; not to operate this way does your people a disservice and allows you to miss out on one of the best time savers managers can find.

82 WORK TO RULE!

MANAGEMENT IN TODAY'S environment necessarily involves consultation; dictatorial management has, by and large, long gone. It makes sense. People will go along much more wholeheartedly with things—policies, practices, whatever—if they feel they have played some part in their origination. At its most powerful this creates what is nowadays called ownership and is a force for commitment and getting results. But there are limits.

If there are no rules, or rules are not applied, then much time may be used up to achieve something that should be simple. For example, having no penalty for failure to get information in on time fails to draw attention to the deadline and provides no incentive for it to be done—or done on time.

The idea

Just because consultation is a good thing, it does not mean that you have to consult, interminably, over every single task. To balance the time this takes, you need other areas where, while the policy is sensibly constituted, there is no debate, no time wasted on it, and things are set up to ensure this is so.

Take the example of form filling. No one likes doing it. In one office the completion of various monthly control documents caused endless, time-consuming problems as deadlines were missed and chasing had to be done. The answer was to link the form completion to the payment of monthly expenses: no form deadline hit, no check that month. The problem—and the time-wasting—went away overnight. In fact, people saw this as reasonable; they knew the system was necessary, the new announcement was well presented, and the results spoke for themselves.

In practice

- The most important thing happening here was that there was a group agreement that certain things simply had to go right without a lot of time being spent to achieve them. The incentive described above is neat and makes it a nice example, but there might be numerous things a manager could do in such circumstances to add a bit of an edge to the rule. The important point is that there should be certain areas where you operate in this sort of way. There is a firm rule, possibly a sanction, and it is clearly understood by all that there will be no exceptions, no excuses, and no time wasted. If something does go wrong having set up things on this basis, then you have to descend from a great height and read the riot act—and do so consistently. The quid pro quo of all this is that, by not endlessly debating or avoiding rules, time is left for consultation on more important issues.

83 A BALANCING ACT

THE ANSWER TO maximizing productivity in your job is not to work longer and longer hours. This may seem like a contradiction in terms. Surely if you put in more hours you will achieve more as a result? Yes, perhaps to an extent you will. The point, however, is that there are limits. The day is fixed at 24 hours for us all; the amount of time we have to work with is finite.

It seems to be one of life's rules that jobs that are interesting are not compatible with a strictly 9–5 attitude; in part, this is probably why they are interesting, so I am not advocating this, though I do believe the long hours culture in some organizations has hit diminishing returns.

The idea

You must strike a balance: that between work and home and outside interests and commitments. If you overdo the work, the other things—and they are important—suffer. What is more, damage, if damage is done, is insidious. You may not be aware of a difficulty until it is too late and begins to cause some real problems. The answer is to consciously seek to strike a balance; indeed, you may want to lay down some rules for yourself about this, specifying maximum hours for work, travel, or spending on specific things.

In practice

- Toward the end of an excessive number of hours, productivity (and concentration) will drop. For those readers who are managers, remember that the overall work capacity of the team you control is very much greater than yours, so it always makes sense to take a team view of things rather than just opting to do more yourself. Finally, excessively long hours worked can be misunderstood and make it appear to others that you are inefficient, which is presumably the reverse of how you want to appear. Long hours will be necessary on some occasions, to complete a particular project, say, but in excess are likely to produce declining standards and run risks that make smarter working a much more attractive option. It is something to ponder (though not late into the night!) in order to make sure that you create a working pattern that is well balanced in this way.

84 AVOID DUPLICATING INFORMATION UNNECESSARILY

MAINTAINING ANY INFORMATIOIN system takes time, and this is multiplied if the information is being recorded in identical or similar form in several different places.

The idea

This is worth a check, and there is a quick check you can run in a few moments. The job you do will give rise to the areas of information with which you are concerned, but, whatever it is, a simple matrix of information shown alongside places where it is filed or stored will quickly show if duplication is occurring.

Such an analysis will also quickly show the extent of any kind of duplication—and the sheer extent of the recording going on. If you then think about where information is most often sought, you may well find that only a minority of places are in fact necessary. Cuts— perhaps recording something once instead of four or five times— will then save work and time.

In practice

Sometimes tasks seem important and then something happens to show that this was not true at all, or perhaps not true any more. This is often the case with information. Something is asked for, is provided regularly, and can continue to be provided long after it has ceased to be useful; it becomes an unquestioning routine.

You should make it a rule that whenever you are asked or need to provide any information to anyone (with copies to whomever else), you make a diary note to check at some time in the future—in six or 12 months perhaps—whether it is still necessary. Find out whether it still needs to be sent:

- On the same frequency (would quarterly be as good as monthly?).

- To all the people originally listed.

- In as much detail (would some sort of summary do?).

Any change that will save time is worth while and you may find that it is simply not necessary to provide the information any more. Very few people will request that information stops coming to them, but if asked may well admit that they can happily do without it. Be wary of this sort of thing, or it is quite possible that all around your organization, action of this sort is being repeated unnecessarily.

THE RIGHT METHODOLOGY?

ANOTHER USEFUL WAY to ensure you have adequate time for priority tasks is to review how exactly they, and other tasks too for that matter, are conducted. Clearly, how you do something—the methodology—affects how long it takes.

The idea

Because of this, there is sense in reviewing working methods on particular tasks and perhaps in doing so regularly. I am not suggesting that you stop all other work and spend time only on an examination of how things are done, but that you set yourself the job of reviewing a series of things over a period of time to search for worthwhile improvements.

In practice

Obviously, the changes that might be made to any task will depend on the nature of the task, but all sorts of things can be worthwhile—for example:

- Systematizing a task that was previously more random or circuitous.

- Changing actual methods.

- Working with someone else: for example, a report might be more quickly finalized if a colleague critiques the draft.

- Lower standards: one method may achieve perfection; another—faster—one may achieve a lesser, but perfectly acceptable, result and sometimes save money.

- Subcontract: in other words, pay an external supplier to do something that they can do quicker, and sometimes cheaper and better, than you.

Again, such a list could go on, and you may be able to think of routes to action that suit your particular job and work best for you. However, the principle of checking to see if there is a better way of doing something is sound. This needs active review and an open mind. Anything you can think of to prompt the process may be worth considering. However it happens, make it happen, for there is never only one right way of doing anything for ever, and improved methodology can be a great time saver.

MAKE SKILLS SAVE TIME

DELEGATION IS REFERRED to elsewhere and is clearly dependent on members of staff actually having the necessary competence to take on whatever may be delegated. Extending capacity throughout a team may thus be dependent on development. Yet development and training all too easily go on the back burner when you are busy.

The idea

So managers should resolve to make training and development a priority (apart from anything else, it is motivational and that pays dividends too). How much time you might save therefore if a member of staff goes on a course, say, and enhances their skills in some way should be as much a consideration as any other; in fact, it's an important one.

In practice

- Remember that training is an ongoing process and that there is a plethora of methods all designed to impart knowledge or develop skills. Some are very simple; your reading this book can be described as development activity, so there are plenty of possibilities. Remember that action here may need to link into various systems such as job appraisal and to other departments such as human resources.

- This can be a classic case of a positive balance: time invested is necessary, but the payoff can often be well worth while. It is a pity if the longer-term nature of the development process makes it less likely to be taken advantage of, because not only will you save time, but it will also lead to the other benefits of more delegation, enhanced motivation, and thus stimulation of the whole process of running the organization.

87 | TIMING AND MEETINGS

TIME IS A resource like any other, one worth conserving and utilizing carefully; the timing element of meetings provides an opportunity to put this directly into practice. For what time do you schedule a meeting, and what other timing implications are there?

The idea

Think what timing factors make a meeting go well. The principles here start with the fact that every meeting needs a starting time. But when that is exactly can affect how productive the meeting will be. Set a time too late in the day and everyone is tired and enthusiasm may well be low; but it will be easier to stop a meeting running on too long. Similarly, if you need a couple of hours for something, then starting at 11:00 a.m. will give you a couple of hours before lunch and again people will be less inclined to encourage the meeting to run on and on.

Perhaps an early start suits. At 8:00 or 8:30 a.m. you may have a quiet hour before the switchboard opens and more interruptions are likely. It depends on the work pattern of your organization and your office, but whatever time you choose it makes a difference.

In practice

Once you are under way, there are other timing factors to worry about—for example:

- *Finishing time*: Every meeting should have not only a start time, but also a finish time. It is a courtesy to people, and helps keep the meeting on track, to set aside a specific amount of time for a session. You can always finish early, and should try hard not to overrun. If you always do this, you will get better at judging how long things need.

- A *timed agenda*: Similarly, it helps to have items on the agenda timed (perhaps not every last one, but certainly main headings and topics). Again this helps focus discussion and will give you something to aim for—"Let's try to get this out of the way in the next 20 minutes." It really helps.

- *Respect for time*: This is especially important and starts right at the beginning. A great time-waster is the common situation where someone is late for a meeting. People congregate, the start time arrives, not everyone is present, it is decided to "wait five minutes," coffee is poured, various ad hoc (and probably not very useful) discussions start among various individuals, time passes, and finally the meeting starts 15 minutes late with someone still to arrive. Ten minutes later, just as things are really getting down to business, the latecomer appears. Apologies and recapping waste another five minutes. If there are, say, eight people at the meeting, this scenario can waste as much as eight times half an hour, that is four hours—sometimes without this even seeming exceptional! Yet imagine the waste in a large department or organization over a year. The moral deserves emphasis: *always start meetings on time*.

The things mentioned here are all important not only in themselves, but as visible signs of your attitude in this area as a potential instiller of good habits. One final word almost goes without saying—it is all helped immeasurably if you are punctual for any meeting you attend, and especially those you have convened!

88 PLAN YOUR JOURNEY

ANY KIND OF disorganization on a journey can waste time. There are a number of considerations here, and it is easy to waste time by overlooking even the basic things.

The idea

Think about every journey you make in advance. Planning is a sensible, and time saving, precaution, and you can usefully consider a number of things in advance.

In practice

Among the areas to consider are:

- *Destination*: For simple and complex journeys alike you need to know exactly where you are going. This helps everything from selecting the best mode of transport to which hotel to stay in once you arrive. It is useful to ask people you are to visit certain questions: for example, in most cities parking is a problem, so before you decide to drive, ask if they have parking spaces. If the answer is "no," taxi or bus may be better, but a "yes" may make driving the best option.

- *Method of transport*: Depending on the destination, there may be a considerable choice: car, taxi, bus, or train; or you may have to fly for longer distances. More complex journeys involve additional decisions—for example, what is the best way into town from the airport? The most comfortable is not always the quickest, of course, and you may be better sacrificing your comfort to take the bus.

- *Route*: This needs deciding also. The greatest time saver here is to combine tasks that involve the same journey or are en route. If I am traveling from London to Singapore, I cannot do this every day and have to think about putting together a group of activities to make the time away worth while, and may also think about whether it would be time-effective to stop en route—in Kuala Lumpur or Bangkok perhaps—or go onward to Hong Kong as part of the same trip, as two separate trips will always be more time-consuming. It is just as worth while thinking and organizing like this if you are going to the other side of town rather than a long distance.

- *Class*: Here again you must balance comfort and cost, but greater comfort can allow more work to be done en route or enable you to get down to work faster on arrival. For many, the very considerable extra cost of even business class over economy on the airlines means careful thought is needed. You will be even fresher if on a long journey you have an extra day in a reasonable hotel before you go to work. This costs a fraction of the difference on the air ticket between classes but takes up more time.

- *Personal/business motivation*: A warning: sometimes decisions are made that produce personal advantage but waste time. For instance, traveling a route that gives you points on an airline loyalty scheme, rather than a faster route.

- *Packing*: Remember that traveling light can certainly save time (particularly if you have no check-in baggage when you fly), and you can get around more easily and quickly if you are not burdened with heavy luggage. But you must also make sure you have everything with you that you may need, to avoid wasting time. You cannot just grab a calculator or find a file in the next-door office.

Developing some good habits, even some checklists, can be useful. The better you arrange a journey, the less it will disrupt other activities. If you travel regularly, you will be able to take advantage of some time-saving perks that the airlines and other travel providers offer to their frequent users; these include fast check-in, transport to the airport, later hotel check-out times, etc. Such things are worth keeping an eye open for, as anything that reduces the time on a journey even a little may be worth while—especially if it also removes some of the hassle.

WORKING THE PLAN

TASKS MUST BE noted not just as a list of "things to do," but in the right kind of way followed by regular review.

The idea

Your "to do" list can usefully follow a pattern that, as a memory jogger, I have heard described as the LEAD system, with the letters of the word "lead" standing for:

- List the activities; this must be done comprehensively, though in note form as you do not want the list to become unmanageable.

- Estimate how long each task will take as accurately as possible.

- Allow time for contingency as things always have a potential for taking longer than your best estimates (remember this is one of Murphy's famous laws); also allow time for regular tasks, the ongoing things that continue routinely day by day.

- Decide priorities; this is referred to elsewhere and is crucial.

Scan the plan, reviewing it overall probably once a day. (When I am in my office I like to do this at the end of each day, updating in the light of what has gone on during the day, followed by a quick review at the start of the next day when the mail arrives and I first check email. But what matters is what you find suits you.)

In practice

- This process should become a routine. What other action may be necessary will depend on the pattern of your day and work.

Something cropping up during the day may be either thought about and added to the list at the time or simply put on one side to be incorporated into the plan at the next review (something like 3M's Post-it Notes are useful for making a brief note of something, sticking them to your planning sheet, and then incorporating them in more permanent form later).

- This review and recording cycle is the heartland of time management, whether you use a proprietary time management system or a home-devised one. A sheet ruled into a number of spaces or the use of a second colour, or both, can make what may well be a full list easier to follow. If items are reliably listed and the list conscientiously reviewed, then you will keep on top of things and certainly nothing should be forgotten.

90 ALLOW FOR THE UNEXPECTED

WHATEVER YOUR JOB, some tasks are likely straightforward. They consist essentially of one thing, and all that matters is deciding when to complete them and getting them done. But many tasks are made up of a number of stages that may be different things you do yourself or do with other people. In addition, some stages may be conducted in different locations and the whole process may take days, weeks, or months. All of which makes it important to schedule such multistage things in the right way if all priority tasks are to be completed on time. What can happen is that you take on a project and begin by feeling it is straightforward, but then find that it is rather more complex.

Consider an example: you are to produce some sort of newsletter. Let us say this is done in four stages: deciding the content, writing it, designing it, and printing it. You complete stage one and stage two, but at this point it has taken somewhat longer than you thought. You hasten into stage three, but halfway through it becomes clear that the complete job will not be finished on time. At that point it may be possible to speed things up, but other priorities could suffer, or the only way to hit the deadline may then be to use additional help, spend additional money, or both.

The idea

What needs to be done is to approach scheduling from the end of the cycle. Start with the deadline, estimate the time spent on each stage, make sure that the total job fits into the total time available, and *allow sufficient time for contingencies*—things cannot always be expected to go exactly according to plan.

In practice

- Furthermore, do not look at one thing in isolation: see how something will fit in with or affect other current projects and responsibilities. It may be that you need to adjust the way stages work to fit with other matters that are in progress. For example, perhaps one part can be delegated so that this is ready to enable you to pick up the project and take it through to the end.

- A variety of options may be possible early on, whereas once you are partway through a task the options may well decline in number and the likelihood of other things being affected increases. All that is necessary here is that sufficient planning time precedes the project, and that in thinking it through you see the overall picture rather than judging whatever it is as a whole and oversimplifying it by just saying "No problem" as you take something on.

91 | SO CATS CAN PLAY

WHAT HAPPENS WHEN you are away from your office? If the wrong things are sent to you, it wastes time; if the wrong things are held back or, worse, handled incorrectly in your absence, then more time will be wasted.

The idea

Wherever you go, whatever the specific purpose of any trip, you need a system to keep you in touch. Such a system starts, therefore, with the briefing of other people in your office, especially your secretary/ PA if you have one. If you do not say what current priorities are and how things should be handled while you are away, then things have no hope of running smoothly. Modern communication makes things easier and long-distance absences create fewer problems as a result.

In practice

Keeping in touch is a two-way process. You need to contact your office regularly, and the information you give must be precise if instructions are to be followed accurately. Remember that people can only know what you tell them and long-distance misunderstandings may take longer to sort out. And do not forget the basics:

- Leave a note of all your contact addresses and other details.

- Advise when you can be contacted and when not.

- Advise any changes to your arrangements as you go along.

- Give an idea in advance of the workload you will bring back for others on your return and the urgency of such tasks.

This is less an area of time saving than of making sure that time is not wasted because of lack of contact and information. Finally, with this sort of organization, there should be no need to keep telephoning, as many people do, just to say, *Is everything all right?* If there is anything to tell you, organize things so that you'll hear.

92 COPING WITH IT CHANGE

A SHORT SECTION made necessary by today's high-tech and fast-moving society: things change and nowhere quicker than in the world of information technology (IT). When I last upgraded my laptop computer, its contents were downloaded ready to go into the new one, which I was assured would then function exactly like my old one. The process took an hour and 20 minutes. The new one sucked all that in over just three minutes; that's how much things had changed in the three years between computers.

The idea

Review, regularly and systematically, all the IT equipment you use.

In practice

Any examples will quickly date, no doubt, but the following still make a point. Consider:

- Computers (for example, having a laptop to improve productivity on the move is now a lot easier because costs have come down so much—as I write, you can even get a free laptop with a cellphone).

- Portable memory (you can effectively carry most of your life in something the size of a cigarette lighter; this reduces time spent on communication to and fro).

- Cellphones (which will collect your email and help you when you are lost).

- Dongles (which can link your laptop to the internet almost anywhere).

Enough; as I said, all this will date. The point remains, however, that many changes and improvements provide features that can save you time. There are costs involved (and a learning curve), but keeping up to date technologically can certainly help you maximize the effectiveness of your time management.

TIME TO TELL A WHITE LIE?

IF YOU ARE 100 percent honest, you may want to skip this section (and get in touch with *Guinness World Records*). Otherwise we might admit that there are occasions when the only way to save time is to be less than honest. Now let me be clear: I am not suggesting that you lie blatantly and persistently through your teeth—indeed, doing so and being found out will do little for your reputation—but there are occasions . . .

The idea

Tell the occasional white lie.

One reason for this may be when saying "no"—*I really can't take that on at the moment; I have to finish this report by the end of tomorrow.* It may mean refusing a meeting by saying you are already committed. The range of possibilities here is considerable. Sometimes doing something like this will work; overdone, it will get you a reputation for avoidance and become self-defeating.

In practice

As a further example, let's take the question of visitors. Some are essential, some outstay their welcome, and others you know from bitter experience multiply every "just five minutes" by ten. In such circumstances people have been known to:

* Set a stated limit—*I must finish at 10:30; I have to . . .*

- Arrange an interruption: having someone come in or telephone to pull you away from the meeting to something else, emergency or planned.

- Canceling—*I can't meet this afternoon now because* . . . maybe substituting a few minutes on the telephone for a meeting to deal with whatever was planned.

Early in my career I worked for someone whose work involved seeing a great many people from outside the organization. Not all of these meetings were useful, and some turned out to be a waste of time. However, experience had taught him to be a pretty accurate judge in advance of which were going to waste time.

To combat time-wasters he had one of the chairs in his office adapted. The front legs were made just one inch shorter than the back. Now this is not dramatic and it does not show (at least it withstood a normal glance—perhaps people did notice but did not believe it), but it is curiously less comfortable than usual. He always swore that he could measure the amount of time saved as people excused themselves earlier than might otherwise have been the case. I was never quite sure about this—but you never know, maybe it's worth a try, if only for certain persistent offenders.

Certainly it makes sense not to maximize comfort for every visitor. If someone is sitting in an easy chair, drinking the second cup of coffee you insisted on, then they are probably not going in the next two minutes. You cannot say "Goodbye" just as they add the sugar to a full cup. As with so much else, this sort of time wasted adds up over the course of the year. Do not, of course, be unsuitably inhospitable, but think before you overdo it as it could take up more time than you want or the occasion warrants; and that's the truth.

94   ON THE MOVE

IF YOU TRAVEL away from your office to any extent, then it is worth considering how you can put the travel time spent to some use.

The idea

Plan and do some work on the move. This is another potentially very valuable area of time utilization, and while you might need some rest on journeys too, there are sometimes many, many hours involved, some of which can be put to good use and produce greater productivity.

In practice

There are several areas you might well consider:

- *Reading*: It is useful to catch up with all sorts of material, and easy to do as you go along; even a short journey may get a report or other document out of the way.

- *Writing*: This needs suitable conditions, but a good deal can be done (and dictating too, though this is not always fair on those around you, and you may need some privacy).

- *Computer work*: This includes word processing (my own favorite travel occupation). Smaller and smaller laptops, and longer battery life, make this a real possibility, and you quickly get into the habit of doing this kind of work on the move and mentally pushing the surroundings into the background.

- *Discussion*: This is clearly only for when you travel with colleagues. If you do, there is no reason why you cannot schedule a proper meeting complete with agenda. That said, I have occasionally got into discussion with strangers on planes with whom I have ended up working, so maybe it is not only for working with colleagues.

- *Telephoning*: Cellphones make this possible in many circumstances these days (though you should consider the peace and quiet of others). Indeed, with modern equipment, you can send email too and few communications options are impossible.

- *Thinking*: This is particularly useful; you may need no papers, no equipment, only the intention and the plan to do so. I keep in my diary a list of "thinking things," longer-term issues, specifically needing no paperwork, that I can work on when suitable moments occur.

All forms of transport lend themselves to some of these kinds of task. You will get most done on longer journeys, and flying and train journeys provide a better, steadier work surface than a bumpy car ride. The trick is to plan to take suitable work and materials, and, if you note how much you get done, you will give yourself an incentive to do this; it is really very useful. So too is work done in hotels: again this must be fitted in reasonably with other activities, but hours can be gained here, and hotels are increasingly well equipped to facilitate communication.

This is another area of potential good habits. If you get used to working like this, taking the right materials and references with you, then you will find it becomes a natural part of the way you function—and the time saving can be very considerable.

NEVER COMPETE WITH INTERRUPTIONS

MEETINGS, EVEN THOSE that are well planned, are vulnerable to distractions. A variety of time-wasting things can and do take place during meetings. Prevention is clearly best, but you may have to deal (and so does the chair) with everything from tea and coffee being noisily delivered, to people being handed, or leaving to collect or deal with, messages—"Sorry, but I just must attend to this one"— and the ubiquitous cellphone. So, what to do?

The idea

In all cases the best rule is to act so as not to allow the distraction to spoil things.

In practice

- So you should acknowledge the distraction, then wait until it has passed. Take a natural break while the tea and coffee are poured, for instance. A two-minute "stretch" break every now and then will anyway help keep people alert in a long meeting, and prevent individuals causing a disturbance as they have to excuse themselves for a moment.

- If interruptions are managed well, then time wasted will be kept to the minimum and key elements of the meeting—a presentation of some important plan, perhaps—will not lose effectiveness and impact by being only half heard or understood. Thus you will avoid the need for recapping and further explanation, which extends the time still more.

- A good chair will think of such things in advance, time the refreshments to coincide with a natural break (and, ideally, the conclusion of an item on the agenda), make sure that cellphones and bleeping reminder systems are switched off, and see that suitable instructions have been left outside the meeting room about messages.

96 MEETINGS: WHERE TO HOLD THEM

MEETINGS CAN BE so time-consuming that they crop up several times in these pages. Where a meeting is held does make a difference to how well it succeeds, and if you are arranging something there may be a good many options: it may be formal or informal, your office may cope with it, or capacity may mean it must take place elsewhere.

The idea

Think about where a meeting should be held and plan accordingly.

In practice

There are a number of things that need some thought, and several factors reflect directly on how long things take—for example:

- *Comfort*: Too much and everyone falls asleep, but too little and the discomfort will prove disruptive. Things to consider here include not just chairs, but the amount of space available for people and papers, lighting levels, appropriate heating/ventilation, ease of serving refreshments, layout, and shape (a long, narrow room may make people at the back feel left out or render them inaudible, but most meetings of the size discussed here are probably best seated boardroom style or, like King Arthur's knights, at a round table).

- *Distractions*: Remove them. No telephone calls or interruptions (except what is sanctioned; some things really do constitute an emergency). No noise, no enthralling view out across some riveting landscape. Remember, every time someone is distracted and interrupts with "Sorry, can you repeat that?" the meeting takes just a few moments more.

- *In or out of the office?* There are some meetings that warrant the cost, and time, of leaving the office and its distractions behind. As an example, consider a senior planning meeting. It has been said already that often there is never sufficient time for planning, especially long-range thinking. But it is vital—somehow it has to be fitted in or the organization's long-term development can suffer. Perhaps two uninterrupted days would make all the difference, in which case a residential session out of town over a weekend may well be justified. Something that might with the best will in the world proceed in fits and starts over some weeks or months can be concluded satisfactorily in two days. It does not even have to be a weekend to justify this kind of approach, and there may be a variety of reasons that make it desirable, such as the need to hold a meeting on neutral ground. If the venue is chosen carefully, you can have a good businesslike atmosphere and some recreational facilities as well if the time taken also provides motivational advantage. This needs thinking about. You cannot go to a resort every time you call a major meeting, but such an approach not only does have its place but can be time-efficient also.

Give your meetings the right environment and they will go more smoothly; and a meeting that goes smoothly will take less time than one that does not.

A TIME-AWARE TEAM

97

S<small>UCCESSFUL</small> <small>MANAGEMENT</small> is dependent on many things, and there is genuine difficulty in putting them in any sort of rank order. Successful recruitment and selection is, however, certainly one of the key ones, and many other things are, in turn, dependent on it.

Management is usually defined as achieving results through other people (rather than for them), and in a commercial organization the objectives toward which you must work and the ultimate results are primarily economic. It is thus different from the things you do— your executive role—and you are dependent on how well your people perform for the overall results for which you are held responsible. If you recruit the wrong people, nothing else you can do may be able to make up for this, and results will suffer.

The idea

Given people of equal technical ability, then one factor that will condition their success, making it either better or worse, is their productivity; time management affects us all. Recruit time-aware people and your team will perform better.

In practice

- Finding the right people is a skill. Most of us are not inherently able to look people over and make an instant and correct decision as to whether they will perform well or not, however much we might like to think we can. Curiously, people are very myopic in this area, so selection must be a systematic process. It is rather like completing a jigsaw puzzle: gradually, from the application form, interview, observations, and references, you put together a sufficient picture on which to make a judgment. It is never complete, and you need to be aware that most people are putting on their very best face throughout this process. They are unlikely to turn out better than you think and may well be just a little less good.

- Whatever other characteristics you demand (and leaving the considerable complexities of this on one side), consider adding time management skills. Candidates will display some—or should. Are they on time for the interview? Has any deadline for the receipt of applications been met? Is their application form legibly and completely filled in (avoiding time being wasted in checking)? You may want to ask them questions about how they organize themselves. I do not suggest this is easy, that there is any one magic question that will ascertain whether people are good in this way or not, and you may not be able to be certain when you make an appointment that the candidate does have the right characteristics in this respect or not. But to ignore it is irresponsible, and if you are, or succeed in becoming, a good manager of your time you will find it permanently frustrating to be surrounded by people who, whatever their other good characteristics, are a time utilization nightmare.

MORE POSSIBILITIES

TIME MANAGEMENT IS a perennial issue. But it is also an ideas area. There is no definitive list of methodology, and so no end to finding new ways to improve productivity.

The idea

The good time manager resolves to keep searching for new ways forward.

Some of what makes this possible is no more than keeping your eyes open, but you might also usefully consider:

- *Reading more about it.* You do not need to adopt the physical systems recommended (and sold) in some books unless you want, but they may still have ideas you can use without that. There are articles published regularly in management journals too for which it may be worth keeping an eye open.

- *Attending a—short—course* (or have one run for your company or department). Again this can act as a catalyst and help relate some of the principles to the specific issues that have to be tackled in your own organization. Just a day can be worth while and prompt change.

- *Simply watching others.* There is no monopoly on good ideas and you may spot things others do as being useful for you. If you have colleagues or friends who appear to have a particularly good approach or system, ask them about the way they work— by definition they should have time to spend a moment telling you about it! This may be one of the best continuing ways of collecting further ideas and fine-tuning what you do.

In practice

- Time is short and realistically you are unlikely to do all this, but you are reading this book and that can act as a catalyst. If so, there may be things you want to do now, at once, or certainly put on your list, that will change your working practice. If so, do so. Do not let the moment pass. In the longer term, if it helps foster a habit of inquiry about sources of increased efficiency, that too may well be useful.

- Collecting and testing ideas should be an ongoing process. Keep a list. Try having a short brainstorming session at departmental meetings, exchange ideas, and search for new ones. Hold a competition. Make it an active issue and prompt people to think about their time on a continuing basis. Think of this process as never stopping and you can go on improving your time utilization throughout your career.

FOCUS ON WHAT ACHIEVES RESULTS

AT THE RISK of repetition, because this has tacitly been said in various ways, here's a very brief thought as the penultimate idea. It is one that is common sense, yet is often ignored, and that, if kept firmly in mind, can dictate overall work practices that ensure you are time-efficient and effective.

The idea

The idea is simple (and perhaps in danger of being a cliché, but don't let that stop you heeding it)—never confuse activity with achievement.

In practice

- Most people (all of us?) are paid not for being busy, not even really for doing the things we do, but for what our efforts achieve. If you are tasked with generating ideas, improving productivity, bringing in revenue—whatever—then that is likely to be how you are measured . . . and rewarded.

- It is how you must measure and judge yourself too. Note the achievements. Note what makes them possible, heed the 80/20 rule, and you will perform successfully. Being a good time manager is just part of what makes that possible; but it's an important part.

100 FOLLOW SINATRA

THIS MAKES A strong final point. Time management is a process, one that demands discipline. It does not just happen and it demands a conscious approach. But it is not one rigid set of rules, rather one of many ideas and approaches. So, if you are reading this last, you may have found some ideas that you can use, immediately and directly, some that you will have rejected as clearly not for you, and also areas that require further thinking.

Fine: time management may be something that you have to fight with yourself to implement and that constitutes a battle you will never fully win, but, whatever you decide to do, it must fit in with the way you work. Unless this is so, you will be in danger of the process itself taking over, and of ending up constantly thinking too much about what you should be doing rather than actually doing it. There is an important caveat here. Do not allow the discomfort of some aspects of time management to become an excuse for not having a proper way of tackling things. It is all too easy to end up feeling that to muddle through is in fact quicker in the long run (though it most often is not) and resisting or avoiding any system or approaches that will streamline the way you work.

The idea

You must utilize things, deploy them appropriately, and—do it your way.

In practice

- Realistically, there is a balance to be struck. If you set yourself a convoluted way of working, then, however efficient it might be, it will likely be so uncomfortable that you will never use it properly. But nor, for want of fitting them to the way you work, should you leave out thinking, ideas, systems, and processes that can help you be more effective. As long as you recognize that the overriding tendency among many people is to allow their existing habits to prevail, and see the danger in that, then you can actively work out a set of approaches and create new habits, if necessary, that suit you.

- Do not worry that some things recommended here and elsewhere do not fit for you (as long as you are sure that they don't). Create your own way forward, do it your way, and stick with that. This, and the habit of seeing the search for new ideas as never ending, will let you maximize time utilization in your job.

APPENDIX 1:
CHAIRING A MEETING

You may well have noticed that how well or badly a meeting goes is usually a direct reflection of the capabilities of the chair, and, if no one is in the chair, the thing is usually a muddle from beginning to end. You are not going to help your cause in time management without the ability not only to attend a meeting and perform impressively, but also to chair one.

For the managing director at least, position and authority will work in their favor to keep things going well in some respects. Down the line, it is perfectly possible to find yourself chairing a meeting where some of those attending are more senior and more experienced than you. So it is an area where, though practice of course helps, you have to make a good start. Therefore it is another skill worth researching and learning to excel at; certainly it is one with a direct link to time utilization.

For example, the chair must:

- Be prepared (preferably more thoroughly prepared than others attending).

- Set and keep to the agenda and keep time (an ability to run to time is especially impressive to others).

- Keep control, yet encourage discussion, let people have their say, and comply with any rules.

- Be able to field questions, arbitrate in debate, and referee in argument.

- See, and deal with, both sides of the case.

- Summarize clearly.

- Arbitrate where necessary.

- Prompt and record decisions and maintain a reasonable consensus.

Resolve to be a good chair, acquire the skills to be so, and use them fairly, as being in the chair is not about riding roughshod over everyone by sheer weight. Apart from anything else, others will resent the roughshod approach. Get things done, but get people feeling that decisions made are good decisions, sensibly arrived at, and that they contributed to the process, and they will be queuing up to attend your meetings, not least because they don't waste time!

APPENDIX 2: DELEGATING

Don't do it—delegate. This too was mentioned in the text. It is a major area of time saving for anyone managing a group of people and thus is returned to and investigated here in more depth.

If a task simply has to be done, but you cannot get to it, then the best way to give yourself more time is to delegate the doing of it to someone else. This is eminently desirable and yet, for some, curiously difficult. First, consider the advantages, and do this by asking yourself what sort of manager you would want to work for. You could probably list a great many qualities: someone who is fair, who listens, who is decisive, good at their job, and so on—but I would bet you put someone who delegates high on the list. The opposite is a boss who hangs on to everything, does not involve you, is probably secretive, and generally is not the sort of person you would want to work for at all. So, if you delegate effectively, there are major advantages in other ways: motivation and the chance to tackle new things for one, as well as the time you will save.

Second, let us look at the difficulties. Delegating is a risk. Something may go wrong, and what is more, as the manager, you may be blamed. So, despite the fact that going about it the right way will minimize the risk, there is temptation to hang on to things. This makes for problems in two ways. You have too much to do, and particularly too much at the more routine end, keeping you from giving the attention you know they deserve to things that are clear priorities. And people do not like it; so motivation— and productivity on the things they are doing—will also be adversely affected.

But there is another important and significant reason why delegation sometimes does not happen. This is fear, not that the other person will not be able to cope, but that they will cope too well, that they will improve the method, that they will do things more quickly, more thoroughly, and better in some way than you. If you are honest, you may admit this is a real fear too; certainly it is as common as the fear that other people will not cope. But it is not a reason that should put you off delegating—the potential rewards are too great.

The amount you can get done if you delegate successfully is way beyond the improvement in productivity you can hope to achieve by any other means. So it is a vital area. But what about something delegated that does go better? So much to the good: this is one of the key ways that progress is made in organizations as new people, new methods, and new thinking are brought to bear on tasks. Without it, organizations would become stultified and unable to cope with change. And, besides, as the manager you should be the reason they are able to make this happen. It is your selection, development, counseling and management that create and maintain a strong and effective team; and this is something for which you deserve credit.

All that is necessary to make delegation successful is a considered and systematic approach to the process. Such an approach is now reviewed. Let there be no doubt just how important this is. What does successful delegation achieve? There are five key results—see page 155 for the full list.

Yet, despite such advantages, it can be curiously difficult to delegate, and there are some managers who find it impossible—and it does carry risks. But the risks can be minimized.

Minimizing the risks

There is always the possibility that delegation will not work. After all, when you delegate, you pass on the right to be wrong, as it were, by putting someone else in the driving seat. So, if a misjudgment is made about the choice of what is to be delegated, to whom it is to be delegated, or how the process will be carried out, things may end up with mistakes being made, and time being wasted as a result.

So you must act to minimize the inherent risks, first by selecting tasks that are suitable for delegation. In most management jobs there will be certain things that should sensibly be omitted. These include:

- Matters key to overall results generation or control.

- Staff discipline matters.

- Certain contentious issues (e.g., staff grievances).

- Confidential matters (though be sure they need to be confidential; protecting unnecessary secrets can be very time-wasting and often fruitless).

Then, in picking the best person to whom to delegate, you should ask questions such as:

- Have they undertaken similar tasks in the past?

- Do they have the necessary knowledge, experience, and capability?

- Is the task too much to cope with at once?

- Is prior training (however informal) necessary?

- Do they want to do more? (Or should they?)

- Will they be acceptable to others involved and will it be accepted also as a fair opportunity among peers?

Thereafter, perhaps the greatest guarantee of success is clear communication, and that does not just mean with the person involved, but more widely as necessary. Others may have to know what is going on and have to trust in the person's ability to do something. Messages may need to be passed up and down and across the line to ensure total clarity. Make sure there is nothing left out regarding authority or responsibility, and that, above all, the individual concerned knows why the job is necessary and why they are doing it. And, as the result of giving a clear brief, you can be confident that they are able to do it satisfactorily.

Any explanation needs to make clear whether what is being done is a one-off exercise, perhaps in an emergency situation, or ultimately a permanent addition to their existing set of responsibilities. Remember, delegation is more than simple work allocation and has implications for such matters as job descriptions and even salary and employment conditions. Assuming that delegation is well chosen and communicated, the next step is to keep in touch, at least initially, with how things are going.

Monitoring progress

Once something has been passed over, keeping in touch can easily be forgotten, and when done can present certain problems. It must be done, in a word, carefully. If it is not, then it will smack of interference and may doom the whole process.

The simplest way to monitor in an acceptable manner is to build in any necessary checks at the time of the original briefing and handover. From the beginning, ask for interim reports at logical points. Do not simply arrive unannounced at someone's desk and ask to see the file (they may be at an awkward stage). Let them bring things to you, and to an agreed deadline. If they have been well briefed, know what is expected, and to what standards, then they can deliver in a way that either duplicates past practice or brings something new to the activity. Either may be appropriate in the short term, though, as nothing lasts for ever; new thinking is usually to be encouraged once the person has a real handle on the basics.

It may be necessary to let things proceed, to bite your tongue, and resist taking the whole matter back as you see things proceeding in a way that may well differ, if only a little, from the way in which you would have done the job. The ultimate results make all this worth while, and not just in time terms but in terms of growth and development within the workplace.

So far so good; if all goes well, surely there is nothing more to be done? Wrong. The process must be evaluated.

Evaluating how delegation has worked

Once sufficient time has gone by and you can assess how things have gone, a number of questions should be asked. These can usefully include:

- Has the task been completed satisfactorily?

- Did it take an acceptable amount of time?

- Does it indicate the person concerned could do more?

- Are there other tasks that could be delegated along the same route?

- What has been the effect on others? (For example, are others wanting more responsibility?)

- Is there any documentation change necessary as a result?

- Has any new or revised methodology been created and are there implications arising from this (e.g., a change to standing instructions)?

- Overall, what has the effect been on productivity?

This last question brings us to a key aspect of evaluation: what has the effect been on you? In other words: what have you done with the time saved? (It might have enabled you to take on new work or facilitated a greater focus on key or long-term issues.)

You will gain little by delegating if you only end up submerged in more detail and have little or nothing of real substance to show for the change. Similarly, should the process not be a success, questions should be asked about what went wrong and they too need to address both sides, asking not just what did someone else do wrong or misunderstand, but also raising such questions as how thoroughly you in fact briefed that person. It is important to learn from the experience; testing what you delegate, to whom, and seeking the best way of handling the process is well worth while. If you develop good habits in this area, it can pay dividends over time.

At the end of the day, the effect on others is as important as the effect on you. People carry out with the greatest enthusiasm and care those things for which they have responsibility. In delegating, you pass on the opportunity for additional responsibility (strictly speaking, responsibility can only be taken—you cannot force it on people) and you must also pass on with it the authority to act. As has been said, delegation fosters a good working relationship around a team of people. Not least, it produces challenges, and, though there are risks, people will normally strive hard to make it work and the failure rate will thus be low. Certainly the effect on productivity can be marked. But—there is always a "but" with anything of this sort—it is a process that needs care, determination, and perhaps even sacrifice. Delegation is not just a way of getting rid of the things you regard as chores—among the matters most likely to benefit from delegation are almost certainly things you enjoy doing.

The potential rewards cannot be overrated, and the need to make delegation work is therefore strong—for the manager wanting to be a good time manager it is crucial. The two things go together. You cannot be good at time management if you are poor at delegation.

This is an area to think on. Do you delegate? Do you delegate the right things and do it sufficiently often? How well does it work? While the principles reviewed here are important and it is something to be tackled on the right basis, an intention and commitment to making it work are perhaps even more important. It may be worth more time to check it out. If you think there is more that you could delegate, review just what and just how you can action the process to get the very most from it in terms of your time and all the other advantages that can flow from it. Perhaps you should consider attending a course on delegating (or better still, send your assistant!).

Delegation can make a major contribution to effective time management. Yet, as we have seen, this is an area of multiple tactics; many things can contribute positively—and much time saved as a result of working at it as an ongoing process.

Eternity is a terrible thought. I mean, where is it going to end?

Tom Stoppard

OTHER 100 GREAT IDEAS

100 Great Sales Ideas
From leading companies around the world
Patrick Forsyth

**Do you "climb the stairs" to find new clients? Do you have a
spoken logo? And how do you cope when you meet that prospect
you just can't get along with?**

Selling—the personal interaction between buyer and seller—is
a key part of the overall marketing process. However much
interest other marketing has generated, selling must convert
that interest and turn it into action to buy. In today's market a
key issue is to differentiate, to ensure your approach sets you
apart from competition. A creative attitude to sales activity
is even more important when faced with difficult markets or
economic times.

Selling success can be made more certain if you adopt an active
approach, understand the way it works, and deploy the right
techniques in the right way. *100 Great Sales Ideas* will help
you achieve that success by providing a resource to assist the
continuous process of analysis and review that is necessary to
create sales excellence.

This book holds 100 self-contained sales ideas from companies
as varied as Raffles Hotel (Singapore), Sony and Amazon, with
observations from Cathay Pacific Airways and Waterstone's
bookshops. It also reveals that one new idea may take you a
step forward in terms of results and customer satisfaction but a
steady stream of them will secure your future.

ISBN 978-0-462-09961-3 / £8.99 PAPERBACK